Inside you'll meet . . .

Angus, the beloved Labrador retriever, whose name has been immortalized by his master, a stained-glass artist, in the National Cathedral in Washington, D.C., and in cathedral windows up and down the eastern seaboard.

Patches, the collie-malamute who jumped into the icy waters of Washington State's Lake Spanaway three times before successfully towing his owner to safety.

Bobby, the young mutt so devoted, he lay on his master's grave for over a decade, until his own death.

Brownie, a stray adopted by an entire street of merchants; he lived happily and independently for fifteen years. His headstone in Daytona Beach says it all: "Brownie 1939–1954. A good dog."

Woodie, the stubby little collie-mix who leaped down an eighty-foot cliff, crushing her hip, and remained at the side of her unconscious owner until help arrived.

Rex, the U.S. Marine dog, who was credited with saving 150 American lives in World War II and awarded the American War Dog Medal—the highest award for war dogs. When he died at the age of sixteen, he was given a full military funeral, and to this day an unknown Marine cares for his grave.

Our Best Friends

Wagging Tales to
Warm the Heart

Michael Capuzzo
&
Teresa Banik Capuzzo

BANTAM BOOKS
NEW YORK   TORONTO   LONDON   SYDNEY   AUCKLAND

OUR BEST FRIENDS
A Bantam Book

PUBLISHING HISTORY
Bantam hardcover edition published March 1998
Bantam paperback edition / July 1999

ISBN 978-0-553-76231-0

Published simultaneously in the United States and Canada

Bantam Books are published by Bantam Books, a division of
Bantam Doubleday Dell Publishing Group, Inc. Its
trademark, consisting of the words "Bantam Books" and the
portrayal of a rooster, is Registered in U.S. Patent and
Trademark Office and in other countries. Marca Registrada.
Bantam Books, 1540 Broadway, New York, New York
10036.

146684614

Contents

Introduction

Dogs do something to the human heart. Exactly what that something is can best be described as call-it-what-you-will, but even without a clear definition it does happen. Perhaps, after all the heart rate and blood pressure stats are in, we still have to go beyond to where the heart and the mind reach a mystical confluence like a vast river system in our soul. What dogs do to our heart, apparently, is really a kind of sweetening.

Every love poem, every love letter is an exaggeration. People don't really die for the want of the company of another; it is unlikely that a lover goes months thinking of nothing else. (It would be dangerous to cross the street or even cook much less drive if that were true.) But hyperbole is the stuff of emotions. It is a legitimate effort to express feelings for which our vocabulary is deficient. And so it is with our pets, our interactions with them, and our very fond memories of them. The Capuzzos explore this in anecdote and fond recall by all sorts of people.

With dogs, life is sweeter, we are sweeter for it. (Don't ever try to explain all of this to anyone who hasn't let it happen to them. They will just stare at you.) But if you are a member of the tribe, you are about to take a marvelous journey as Mike and Teresa

Capuzzo, ardent, orthodox, industrial-strength dog lovers, tell you about the absolutely wonderful stories they have uncovered in their travels. Loosen your tie, kick off your shoes, and treat what comes next the same way you treat your dog—with an open mind, lower blood pressure, and gratitude for being able to participate in one of mankind's greatest wonders.

—Roger A. Caras
Thistle Hill Farm

CHAPTER ONE

On Love

Nietzsche said the beautiful words, "Let it be your aim always to love more than the other, never to be the second." With human beings, I am sometimes able to fulfil this commandment, but in my relations with a faithful dog, I am always the second. Have you ever thought how extraordinary is all this? Man, endowed with reason and a highly developed sense of moral responsibility, whose finest and noblest belief is the religion of brotherly love, in this very respect falls short of the carnivores. . . . The plain fact that my dog loves me more than I love him is undeniable and always fills me with a certain feeling of shame.

—**Konrad Lorenz**

A dog is the only thing on Earth that loves you more than you love yourself.

—**Josh Billings**

Qui me amat, amat et canem meum. ("Love me, love my dog.")

—St. Bernard, "Sermo Primus" (1150)

He wasn't the best, but he was the best I ever had.

—Epitaph to Track, buried in the Coon Dog Memorial Graveyard, Colbert County, Alabama

A Dog's Home Is Many Hearths

In 1940, Mickey Mantle turned eight years old. The sounds of swing and bebop were spinning on turntables and the number one best-seller at the bookstores was *Native Son*.

America was relatively lazy and peaceful in 1940. This was especially true in Daytona Beach, a resort city on Florida's northeast coast known for its twenty-three miles of hard, white sandy beaches.

Down on Beach Street, which was the main drag, Ed Budgen ran the Daytona Cab Company. It was neighbor to a bar, a Liggett's drugstore, a barbershop, a pool hall, and a bank.

A yacht marina sat across from the cabstand on the southeast side of Beach Street. On the northeast corner was Riverfront Park, a verdant, pleasantly shady spot in which to gaze out at the Intracoastal Waterway.

In 1940, something about this small-town commercial area attracted a stray dog. Nobody knows where he came from or why, but one day a four-legged stranger wandered into town, sniffed around, and liked what he smelled. That day, Daytona Beach's permanent population—22,580—increased by one.

"I was knee-high to a grasshopper in 1940, but I remember Brownie as a nice, friendly dog," said Ed Budgen's son George. "My father gave him the name Brownie. He was a short-haired, tan dog, around eighteen inches high. He looked somewhat like a boxer."

Ed took the dog to a local veterinarian to be checked out. The vet guessed that Brownie was a year old.

Ed asked around, but nobody knew anything about a runaway dog with a sweet nature. So Ed, the cabdrivers, and the other merchants along Beach Street decided to adopt Brownie.

Ed constructed a doghouse out of a big cardboard box. And that's where Brownie lived. As each doghouse wore out, Ed made another one. Brownie maintained his lease for the next fourteen years, thirty yards from the corner of Orange and Beach.

Every day, Brownie would lope from merchant to merchant. He'd even go into the post office, then cross over to the park and marina.

His visits created an air of comforting consistency. The merchants found themselves expecting—and enjoying—Brownie's presence. As long as he was around to wag his hello, all seemed right with the small world of Daytona Beach.

Brownie became a familiar, welcome fixture in town. Local residents would greet him with a smile, a hug, or a pat. They'd tell him he was a good dog. They'd offer him a treat. And, once in a while, someone would bring him a steak.

E. B. Davidson, who was six in 1940, said, "Brownie loved it when all the kids visited him after school. He was a real nice dog. He had a big head and a long nose. His face reminded me of a Rhodesian Ridgeback, but his body looked more like a hound."

Vince Clarida was a boy when Brownie first came to town. His memories of Brownie include the local patrolman walking his beat along Beach Street—and Brownie tagging along.

"Ed and the other cabdrivers used to feed Brownie a daily pint of ice cream," Clarida said. "That dog loved ice cream!" Ed Budgen fashioned a small pouch or box that he tied around Brownie's neck. It served as a donation box. Residents and winter visitors would drop money into the box. Ed would deposit the money into a special bank account he had opened to help pay for Brownie's food and veterinary care.

Brownie was also famous for constantly crossing into traffic. To the residents' amazement, he was injured only once. It was a leg injury, and it healed.

Brownie was too independent to go home with anyone. But he was attached enough to the people of Daytona Beach to want to live out his years with them.

In October of 1954, Brownie died. Everyone assumed he died of old age. Someone from back home reported the sad news to E. B. Davidson while he was away at college. Neither he nor George Budgen, who was away in the military, could attend the funeral.

"The money in Brownie's bank account paid for the plywood casket and the headstone," Vince Clarida said. "Around seventy-five people were at the funeral, but a lot more people said they'd have been there, too, if they had known."

Mayor Jack Tamm gave the eulogy, in which he declared that Brownie was a good dog. And that's what they all decided to put on the headstone.

There's a cool, quiet spot of grass in Riverfront Park that has a clear view of the calm Intracoastal Waterway at one end and the stores of Beach Street on the other.

Brownie is buried there. His grave is flanked by delicate red flowers. It's covered with a granite stone etched with the likeness of a dog of unknown origin who might have understood that a lot of people loved him.

The granite is cold, but the engraved words are warm: "Brownie. 1939–1954. A good dog."

—Roberta Sandler

Maxie

I remember the first time I saw you at a farm in North Carolina, one little black-and-white face in a group of nine. You saw me, you walked over to me, you picked me. That was the beginning of a ten-year friendship like none I have ever known or experienced.

Our relationship started in Goldsboro, North Carolina, and ended up here in Seattle. As we made our journey from North Carolina to Minnesota to California to Arizona, and then to Washington, the only thing we needed was each other, that along with a job from time to time to keep us warm and our stomachs full. I remember a painful time in my life when I had to leave you with my parents for two years. I never stopped thinking about you and took comfort in knowing you were loved and cared for. I'll also never forget how you knew me the moment you saw me when I came back to get you, and from that moment on, I swore we were never to be parted again.

You gave meaning to each and every day that you were with me, comforted me when I was sad, inspired me when I was confused, loved me when I felt I had no love. I never again thought about not having you with me forever, but I feel I never took the time we did have together for granted. I thank God that you found me, and I have been made richer by the experience.

I knew it was time to finally let you go when you were suffering from brain tumors. The idea of letting you go pained me more than anything I had ever felt before. I was racked with guilt and pain, and I'm sorry I couldn't hide that from you. But I also know that you understood; and that night, as you looked at me in my eyes, you also knew what was happening. I let you go, Maxie, because I loved you, but my memory of you is something I will cling to till the day I die. You continue to comfort me; and though I long to hold you again, I can close my eyes and feel you and know that you are near.

—Anonymous from the Virtual Pet Cemetery

The Never-Ending Dog

Once in south Florida there was a little girl named Jill Francisco. When she was born there was a dog, George, at her side. George was a small shaggy dog who had always slept in Mom's bed. But when Jill was born it seemed like George knew he had a different purpose now.

Each day George would lie by the baby's crib. Every time Jill cried, George howled. When Mom's boss came to see the baby, George almost bit her when she tried to pick Jill up. That was okay; George knew that Mom didn't like her boss.

George was one of Jill's first words. When Jill became a little girl, five years old, George was her best friend. As time went on, Jill went to school and became so busy she paid less attention to George. "We seemed to grow apart," Jill remembered. "But I still loved him. I just didn't show it as much."

When she got older, Jill was so involved with her friends she didn't see much of George at all. George was slowing down then, but he always ran to see Jill whenever she came home, wagging his tail so happily. "I still fed him ice cream when my mom wasn't looking," Jill said.

When George was fifteen years old, and Jill was twelve, George really started to age. All he did was sleep and bark to go out. Jill was annoyed by George and didn't want to be around him. "Then he got cataracts in both eyes and his legs began to get weak," Jill said. "I wasn't really that worried about him but my mom seemed to be sometimes."

At sixteen, the family began calling him "the never-ending dog." As George aged, he was hard for Jill and Mom to take care of. He slept more and more, but he still wagged his tail whenever he saw Jill.

One morning when Jill was fourteen and George was almost seventeen, Jill heard her mom, Denise, say, "I think it's time. All he does is lie on the floor shaking." Jill thought she had outgrown George, but in that moment when she ran with tears in her eyes to her mom and hugged her and said she would help take George to the vet's, Jill knew she was wrong.

Once there was a dog named George. When George lay down for the last time, he had his girl at his side. When George moaned and cried, she cried, too.

"That was the hardest trip I've ever made," Jill told her mother later. "When I went in the room with George and said good-bye to a friend I thought would never leave me. And now I know in my heart he never will. George was my never-ending dog."

—Jill Francisco, age 14

Loving Lizzie

Nearly fifteen years ago in New York City a five-month-old shepherd-Lab mix named Lizzie limped into our lives. She was a pathetic bag of bones—mostly broken since she had been hit by a car—and her prospects in life were dim. Initially, she seemed merely to be the latest in a long line of strays Steve and I rescued, nursed back to health, and sent on to good homes. But something in Lizzie's spirit shone: She may have had a mutt body, but she was pedigreed in soul and became the light of our life.

Steve and I are childless, and we obviously understood that Lizzie was not our child. We agree with John Steinbeck, who wrote that it is better to be a first-rate dog than a second-rate human. Nevertheless, Lizzie did indeed become our "baby." In fact, we joked that Lizzie was a daddy's girl; for although I was the primary caregiver and took her on long hikes, the highlight of Lizzie's day was when her daddy came home from work.

As Lizzie matured our relationship also grew. We became more companions than mother and child, much like adult children and parents develop a deepening friendship and respect. I learned as much from her, if not more, as she did from me. Lizzie had an adventurous spirit and philanthropic heart, and our daily park excursions often netted abandoned and abused dogs, cats, rabbits—even a rooster. Lizzie shared our apartment with several litter-trained rabbits, which we moved to the country when we began spending summers in upstate New York. Lizzie loved the country; and we roamed the fields and woods, tracking deer and rabbits, swimming in the creek with the beavers, and camping outside at night to watch the deer and coyotes. Lizzie's interest in wildlife was purely aesthetic, for she never harmed any animal.

Still Lizzie was at heart a city dog. She loved the hustle and bustle and being sociable and smart; she soon became a neighborhood fixture and was welcomed into shops, churches, delicatessens, and even some restaurants. Indeed her intuitive understanding of people, places, and situations seemed to personify Count Buffon's (France's eighteenth-century "naturalist laureate") observations of how dogs seem to divine and fill the myriad needs of diverse human personalities and their interactions in various familial and societal roles. Lizzie and her rabbits were involved with pet-facilitated therapy projects at a local school for abused children, and she had an innate understanding of and gentleness with elderly and disabled people. Her endearing nature was infectious, and she was invited to many affairs, from local children's parties to society events. I had never cared for big-city living; but Lizzie not only made it more palatable, she made New York City seem like Small Town, U.S.A. With Lizzie, Kitty and Steve Gutstein had become a family.

Recognizing this, when Lizzie turned thirteen, Steve and I wanted to celebrate her life and what she meant to us. Perhaps because our families and friends had celebrated so many weddings, bar mitzvahs, and confirmations (Steve is Jewish, I'm Episcopalian)—or perhaps it was simply because Lizzie was so popular and had so many social obligations to reciprocate—we ended up with two celebrations: We renewed our wedding vows in the bunny yard in the country (Lizzie was the maid of honor, and the guest list included all her bunnies as well as her human and dog friends); and in the city, we had a combination bat mitzvah/confirmation. Although the festivities were at times whimsical and campy, the vows exchanged and verses read were serious and heartfelt.

At fourteen, Lizzie was still rambunctious. Not only had she yet to show her age or signs of slowing down, she had beaten many odds: Medically, she had survived a cancerous spleen, kidney disease, and pneumonia. And because her zest for life took us hiking many miles from home, she accumulated quite a roster of sports injuries. Wearing my belt as a tourniquet, she survived a severed artery; mouth-to-mouth resuscitation revived her after she choked on a chicken bone and passed out; and she recovered after a downed power line wielded a near-fatal shock. With her happy-go-lucky outlook, Lizzie was not only charming but also seemed to lead a charmed existence!

Therefore, it was a devastating day last spring when Lizzie awoke unable to stand. We rushed her to our veterinarian, who diagnosed a debilitating arthritis attack to her hindquarters. The prognosis was extremely guarded, and it was imperative to get her up and around, for if she remained a downed dog she would not survive.

We were instructed to begin by boosting Lizzie into a standing position for a few minutes several times a day (always preceded by massage and range-of-motion therapy). Next, we were to try for a few steps each time we got her standing. This was an extremely tough time for a dog who was not used to lying around housebound. A blessing in disguise turned out to be the pregnant stray cat Lizzie had rescued from the park in a snowstorm just before her arthritis attack. When the kittens were born, they snuggled and played about and upon Lizzie, keeping her entertained and mentally alert. Who could have guessed that kittens would become an important adjunct to Lizzie's medical team?

Still, recovery was a slow and laborious process, with progress being measured in inches, then feet, and finally yards. Sometimes Lizzie fell, but she never appeared bewildered or discouraged, only determined. During this time, I carried a backpack with Lizzie's water, medicine, and an orthopedic mat, so she might rest comfortably whenever necessary. The vets had warned us we would be walking a fine line between too much exercise and not enough. Finally, after eight weeks of intensive therapy, Lizzie was able, albeit gimping somewhat, to walk a few blocks at a time.

Grateful that she had come this far, we turned our thoughts to her quality of life that summer. For Lizzie, summer had always meant hiking, swimming, and camping. We knew Lizzie would expect no less this summer, for despite her arthritis, she was as alert and spirited as ever. Given her physical limitations, how could we give her another such summer? Thankfully, with a little thought, creativity, and effort, we were able to do so.

First, we eschewed her leash and collar, opting instead for a back harness. This gave her support in the hindquarters and a feeling of security; and it helped her avoid the risk of falling and compounding her physical problems. Lizzie took to the harness as though she had always used one. And because steps were an obstacle, we built a ramp into our country house. Slippery floors also posed a problem, because in addition to arthritis, she also suffered from myelopathy, a nerve degeneration of her hindquarters. This problem was easily solved by carpeting all the floors, including the kitchen. Lizzie's pads had also become very sensitive, and she had trouble on the rough country roads and fields. Lizzie was used to wearing a variety of commercial dog boots in the city during winter to protect her from the harsh chemicals, but for her changing needs, they didn't suffice. Because of this and because (as a result of her car injury when she was a pup) one paw was a mangled clubfoot and especially sensitive, we took Lizzie to a number of pedorthists, who design and make shoes and braces for orthopedic patients. After much trial and error, Lizzie had special boots that enabled her to again enjoy country walks. During this time, a veterinarian acupuncturist began working in tandem with our traditional veterinarians, and Lizzie continued to improve.

Next, we constructed a cart for her to ride while we pushed her through the countryside. The cart was built on three mountain-bike wheels, and Lizzie rode three feet off the ground on a hammock-like platform, with extra springs for shock absorption, complete with brakes. We pushed her with handlebars from behind, so her view of deer would not be spoiled. The cart was sturdy and maneuvered easily. With Lizzie perched proudly on the cart like a pampered Roman empress on her throne, we whisked her for miles and hours through her favorite countryside. When she caught a scent to track, she barked to get down and walk. When she had enough, she returned to her "throne," and the adventure would continue. For the city, we built a second, smaller cart, so she could manage walks there, as well.

Now that Lizzie no longer felt secure swimming on her own, and we couldn't risk aggravating her arthritis by getting her wet or chilled, we again improvised. We got a flat-bottomed aluminum fishing boat (dubbed the *Tin Lizzie*, what else?) and built a platform bed on the bow of the boat where Lizzie reclined like Cleopatra sailing up the Nile! The boat allowed Lizzie to again "swim" in the creek and visit the beavers she so adored. For a dog who was always queasy riding in a car, we were amazed and grateful that she so thoroughly enjoyed her boat and cart. Indeed, she positively beamed, and those who saw her commented that she looked half her age. And as for camping out to watch the nocturnal wildlife, that was easy: We simply added an orthopedic mattress and heated blanket to keep her old bones warm and comfortable.

During this, her final summer, we learned that one of Lizzie's kidneys had shut down and the other was badly damaged. Her veterinarian expressed amazement at how well she was functioning despite this. He told us her blood tests showed a very sick dog, but those results were belied by Lizzie's robust behavior. He used the word *miracle* more than once.

And so throughout the summer, until Thanksgiving 1993 when she died peacefully in her sleep in bed with us, Lizzie lived as full a life as she always had. She grew older, but never old, and truly *lived* until she died.

Indeed, in a society that too often worships at the fountain of youth and neglects its elderly, we were blessed to watch Lizzie revel in all the seasons of her life; and her golden years truly shone. We are convinced that Lizzie's indomitable spirit, her zest for life, kept her going. Indeed, she reminded us of Lord Tennyson's Ulysses, who, despite the ravages of old age, was determined to "drink life to the lees":

How dull it is to pause, to make an end,
To rust unburnished, not to shine in use!
As though to breathe were life! . . .

Though much is taken, much abides; and though
We are not now that strength which in old days

Moved earth and heaven, that which we are, we are—
One equal temper of heroic hearts,
Made weak by time and fate, but strong in will
To strive, to seek, to find, and not to yield.

No, Lizzie was not about to yield to disability and illness, not while there were fields and woods to roam, deer and rabbits to track, and beaver-filled creeks to swim. Only after she hiked and tracked and swam; only after she lived that summer to the lees; only after there were no races left for her to run, no adventures left for her to experience; only after she had turned every page in the book of life; only then, with nothing left undone, did Lizzie's remaining kidney fail her.

The months since Lizzie died have been a time to reflect and grieve. While a few questioned the time, effort, and money we expended on this old arthritic dog, the multitude did not, judging by the overwhelming outpouring of cards, flowers, and condolences, many from people whose names and faces we could not place. Those who best understood were the patients and families who shared the pedorthist's waiting room with Lizzie. We worried they would resent Lizzie's presence and our concern for "just" a dog. Surprisingly, they approved unanimously.

All the tangibles we provided Lizzie—the boots, harness, carpets—paid off in intangible returns: Lizzie's happiness. And, as we built ramps, platforms, and carts, we were unwittingly building bridges, for Steve and I were brought closer together; and none of this was lost on Lizzie. She understood what we did for her and appreciated that we did so as a family. Our final summer became our best summer, not only for the joyous times but for the deepening bonds.

Two Shakespearean couplets that Steve read to Lizzie

at our bunny-yard wedding are as apropos today as
then. For when we grieve, it helps to reminisce about
Lizzie:

But if the while I think on thee, dear friend,
All losses are restored and sorrows end.

And as our grief subsides, it can truly be said:

For thy sweet love remembered such wealth brings
That then I scorn to change my state with kings.

—*Kitty Brown Gutstein*

Doggy Baggage

I was a widow in my forties, sharing life with Photon,
my thirteen-year-old miniature dachshund, when I met
Mike. He was a bachelor, nice looking, my age, and a
man my friends said came without baggage.

My friends, however, were wrong. They had over-
looked Tycho, Mike's standard schnauzer. One look at
Tycho, as he elegantly descended from the front seat of
Mike's car, told me that on my driveway stood fifty
pounds of doggy baggage. Not my choice for a pet.
Tycho was too large. He looked too fierce. He needed

grooming. And I could tell that his beard, an obvious dirt collector, was well designed for soaking up water from his bowl and dispersing it across my polished floors.

At first Tycho ignored me, preferring instead to sample unfamiliar scents along the driveway. As I approached Mike, however, he pranced over to inspect me. Positioning himself next to his master, like a chaperon at a dance, he whined his disapproval at our affectionate greeting. Photon, waiting just inside the door, yapped a few times. I glanced at Mike, then into the alert eyes on guard between us. My future was clear. The two of us were not going to forge a new relationship until the four of us formed a new pack.

Blended-dog families, like ours, have become common today. Even dogless people may suddenly find themselves sharing a home with step-pets. These canines are different from puppies we select together and dogs we mutually adopt.

It was hard for me to accept Tycho. I tolerated him, even respected him, but didn't really like him until after he stayed with me for a week while Mike was out of town. I wasn't thrilled, but with only Photon for protection, a serious-looking dog seemed like welcome company. I was also thinking that Tycho and I might have a chance to connect without Mike in the picture. I was right.

One afternoon, while I worked in the garden and Tycho supervised, Photon, who had been sleeping in the sun, wandered off. Nearly blind, totally deaf, and mostly confused, he was incapable of finding his own way home. I left Tycho on a "down stay," and ran off in search of my lost dog. No Photon. Frantic and in tears, I returned to Tycho. Taking his muzzle in my shaking

hands, I repeated a command he was hearing for the
first time. "Find Photon. Find Photon."

I knew that Tycho had never retrieved anything in his
life, and I felt foolish shouting at him. But I was scared,
and he was all the help I had. He responded by tilting
his head and staring at me. "Find Photon," I repeated.
He remained still for a moment, and then moved off
toward the woods. "Oh God," I thought. "Next, he'll
disappear, and then I'll lose Mike, too."

A few minutes later I was startled to hear several
snorts and to see a parade of dogs emerging from the
woods. In the lead was blind little Photon, followed by
Tycho, who occasionally tapped him from behind. I
rushed over to hug Photon and then opened my arms
to take in my step-dog. Tycho responded by rubbing
and sighing and then braggingly prancing about. When
he finally settled himself, he threw a look in my direction that said, "Okay. What next?" I answered with
another hug.

Now, when I look at Tycho, I no longer see fierce
eyebrows and a messy beard. Instead, I see a dog I have
learned to love, a cherished member of my family.

Sometimes, late in the evening, when Tycho is curl-
ing up, ready to fall asleep, I wait for him to look in my
direction one more time. For when he does and his eyes
meet mine, his look will say what we both are thinking:
"Aren't we lucky Mike came with doggy baggage."

—Eleanor Garrell Berger

Sandy

June 23, 1983–October 12, 1996.

When the sun rises over Boundary Butte in southeastern Utah, its first rays strike the dramatic formation called Rooster Rock to illuminate a gold-and-pink beacon of the new day.

Sixty feet below, on a slick rock shelf, visitors share the dawn with a herd of mule deer, who are following an ancient path to a secret oasis; an eagle, who rises from an unseen aerie atop a needle of stone; and the coyotes, who serenaded them to sleep the night before, while the sun slowly sweeps the shadow from the floor of Cataract Canyon.

This was Sandy's last campsite.

Sandy, a cocker spaniel, lived thirteen years, three months, and nineteen days—nearly a hundred human years. For all but his first eight weeks, he was our companion, trailblazer, ward, protector, and best friend.

Sandy died at 11:11 A.M., October 12, 1996, in the Red Rock Animal Hospital in Gallup, New Mexico.

The stoic little animal, who survived life-threatening bouts of Lyme, thyroid, and prostate diseases to climb another mountain and trot another trail, finally succumbed to advanced age and kidney failure.

We were on the road when we met Sandy and, fittingly, when he parted from us.

Sandy was a puppy-farm, pet-shop dog who captured our hearts in a shopping mall in Hyannis, Massachusetts, while we were vacationing. His first home was the cargo area of a Bronco II; and ever afterward, woe betide the gas station attendant or other stranger who came too near whatever vehicle he and his humans occupied.

It was his eyes that won us that first day—big, brown eyes with a vocabulary far richer than mere words. A crusty, nonconformist veterinarian who examined the new puppy thought there was a physical explanation: He put calipers to those eyes and declared that they had a significantly larger bulge than is normal for the breed. I knew the explanation went deeper than that: The windows on Sandy's soul clearly revealed a philosopher. The thought was neither original nor far-fetched: 2,500 years ago, in Book II of his *Republic*, Plato described the dog as "a true philosopher," and Sandy on the trail resembled nothing so much as Plato's philosopher "measuring earth and heaven and all the things which are under and on the earth and above the heaven, interrogating the whole nature of each and all in their entirety."

Once we'd brought him home to Pennsylvania, the shy little creature who'd ridden in the pocket of Lois's jacket and fled the ocean's gentle lapping at the shore on Cape Cod, became our cunning trail dog, trotting tirelessly ahead of us, with an occasional glance back to make sure that we were keeping up or dashing off-trail to interrogate some new aspect of nature. Those excursions we came to call "playing the loop game," for he'd circle around and re-enter the trail behind us, a prank that required professions of great surprise on our part, accompanied by enthusiastic petting and fussing. "Good Sandy!" we'd chant. "Sandy Good Boy!"

There's a dog treat wafer called Good Boy that we used when our puppy was learning *Come* and *Sit* and other basic canine commands, and from that training reward came the mantra Sandy loved to hear. At least once every day of his life he required handling—a carefully scripted ritual of scratching behind the ears and under the muzzle, stroking on back and flanks, and—

grand finale!—a vigorous belly rub as he lay on his back, legs twitching in ecstasy. The mantra "Good Sandy! Sandy Good Boy!" had to be repeated continuously during the stroking ritual.

He had scarcely outgrown the jacket pocket when he made his first nine-mile round trip on the segment of the Appalachian Trail (AT) that leads from the Hamburg Reservoir to the Pinnacle Rocks, the best-known AT landmark in Pennsylvania. That entire section of trail is punctuated by what through-hikers call "the infamous rocks of Pennsylvania," and one quarter-mile stretch just beyond the Pulpit overlook is so strewn with jagged rocks and boulders that many hikers have to scramble on all fours. The bigger rocks must have looked like Everests to the little spaniel the first time he encountered them, but the big brown eyes took on the flinty glint of sheer determination. "Don't slow down," they said. "I can keep up." And, of course, he did.

Some time later, before neutering, when nature aroused his primal instincts, we were utterly baffled by his ability to escape in a trice from our chain-link-fenced, dig-proof backyard in quest of romance. One day we put him out and watched from an upstairs window. Wearing the same determined look we'd seen on the Pinnacle trail, he fitted his paws into the diamond-shaped links and climbed up and over the five-foot fence to go a-courting.

The society of cocker spaniels who have climbed a Colorado "fourteener" must be quite small. Sandy joined it in his seventh September, when, wearing the Pinnacle-trail, fence-climbing look, he led me up a snowy slope of boulders to the unique flat summit of Uncompahgre Peak (elevation 14,309 feet), the highest point in the San Juan range.

He loved the high places. Once, atop Loveland Pass

in Colorado, he yipped in sheer exultation and set off
flying down the mountain, in pursuit of imagined prey
or for the pure exhilaration of it, then struggled back up
the steep hill to flop in a snowbank, panting contentedly. I don't know how many miles he logged on the
AT—hundreds, surely, between Hamburg and the Pinnacle alone—but they took him to the highest points in
a number of eastern states, including Virginia's Mount
Rogers (where he contracted Lyme disease), Connecti-
cut's Bear Mountain, and Massachusetts's Mount
Graylock, and up dozens of challenging mountains in
the Green, Presidential, White, and Blue Ridge chains.
On Pharaoh Peak in the Adirondacks, he had his first—
and only—encounter with a porcupine and bore the
painful shaft-by-shaft removal of the quills without a
whimper, the first evidence of what came to be a storied
stoicism among the veterinarians who treated Sandy
over the years.

He was a favorite patient at Devon Veterinary Hospital where Dr. Carol Caracand's aggressive treatment,
without waiting for blood test confirmation of her intuitive diagnosis of Lyme disease, saved Sandy's life after
hindquarter paralysis had already set in. He was one of
her first canine patients to survive the disease, and she
put him in the literature that persuaded the Pennsylvania Department of Agriculture to approve use of the so-
called Fort Dodge vaccine against Lyme disease. (It
later would prove ineffective.)

Dr. Caracand's associate, Scott Fausel, saw Sandy
through a nearly fatal siege of prostate problems, an
infection that imitated cancer so successfully it fooled a
cytology laboratory—but not Dr. Ann Jeglum, the in-
ternationally known canine oncologist Dr. Fausel consulted.

First-rate veterinary care undoubtedly contributed to

Sandy's longevity beyond a cocker spaniel's normal life span of ten or eleven years. On his last camping trip, his companions benefited as much from the human psychology of two compassionate vets as Sandy benefited from their medical ministrations. Dr. Art Grusensky of Moab, Utah, understood Lois's psychological need to try to get Sandy home before he died and tried heroically to make that possible. When it proved impossible, Dr. Ken Podkonjak at the Red Rock clinic in Gallup treated both Sandy and his grieving companions with a sensitivity and understanding we can never forget.

Sandy was twelve when his failing kidneys were diagnosed at Devon; and although treatment and special diet stabilized his condition, we accepted that he would never again be the trailblazer of old. Some months later, on a winter trip to Florida, a group of friends and relatives set out on a three-mile trek through pine forest to the seashore sand dunes. Sandy was feeling good that day, so I told the others he and I would walk a few hundred yards out with them, then go back to the car to await their return. To my astonishment, he set out ahead of us all in the old, familiar, tail-wagging spaniel strut and never slowed till he'd completed the whole six-mile round trip.

"Sandy, the Bionic Dog," Dr. Fausel said.

Of all the precious memories of that noble little animal, the one I'll carry longest is that of Sandy strutting down a forested trail, interrogating nature for all he was worth.

Trails are longer now, and steeper; I walk them more slowly, and the inner music is more somber than when the wagging tail stub summoned me higher, faster, farther; when the little trailblazer would dart off on the loop game only to surprise me from behind, sprinting

up the path with the spaniel ears flopping like the wings
of some flightless bird; when we'd reach a summit or an
overlook and he'd nuzzle up for his ritual treat and
stroking, for the mantra of "Good Sandy! Sandy Good
Boy!"

Late in October we tried to hike the Dog Canyon
trail in New Mexico, where the insidious cancer impersonator first felled Sandy, and he had to be carried
down by two airmen from Holloman Air Force Base in
a makeshift litter fashioned of hiking staffs and a jacket.
But the air was too heavy with memories there, and we
turned back. In the steep descent at dusk, with no
Sandy to woof a warning, we nearly stepped within
striking range of a rasping rattler coiled at trailside.

"Brothers and sisters, I bid you beware," Kipling
wrote, "of giving your heart to a dog to tear." Yet who,
confronting those remarkably articulate eyes in the pet
shop in Hyannis, could have heeded such a warning? In
the days and weeks since October 1996, we've left
heart-shards scattered across the landscape from New
Mexico to St. David's, but with each grieving beat
comes a rush of joyful memories. Tot up the emotional
accounts and he gave us far more than we gave him.

What fortune could ever buy the nuzzling of an ear
atop Uncompahgre and the loving eyes that said, "See
there, I knew you could make it," even as I gasped for
breath in the oxygen-lean air? I'd never have reached
that summit if Sandy hadn't been there, stoically urging
me up the last steep snowy slope of rock and talus. "It's
a payback," the eyes said, "for that time in Virginia
when you snatched me from the jaws of the bull mastiff
by the waterfall." He was scarcely out of puppyhood
when that happened—a big, ill-tempered beast attack-
ing savagely and without provocation. I reacted instinctively, kicking the attacker's ribs and literally reaching

into its jaws to save my little spaniel. The master of the big dog—a brutish, foul-smelling guy in biker's togs—glowered but said nothing. As I carried Sandy away from there, his big, brown eyes told me, "You're twenty feet tall and no metal can touch me when I'm with you." But the eyes clouded briefly with the after-thought: "Of course, next time, if you could move just a *little bit* faster . . ."

How can I ever walk the paths of Valley Forge with-out remembering the countless early-morning jogs I'd never have taken there but for Sandy's restless urging? I was changing the way I lived when he came into our lives, and part of the process called for more attention to physical fitness. He'd trot beside me on the hills and trails at Valley Forge and Tyler Arboretum, keeping me safe from tigers and bears; and if I'd slow too soon, he'd fix the big, brown eyes on me accusingly: "C'mon," they'd say, "we aren't *there* yet!" On a hillside over-looking Dismal Creek at Tyler there's a plaque on a bench that says, "Sandy's window." It was placed there in memory of some other Sandy, but in his later years, when a leisurely stroll through Tyler was our Sandy's maximum speed, we'd often stop there to rest. I'm sure the other Sandy, whoever he or she was, won't mind sharing the window with ours for the rest of eternity.

How can I ever pitch a tent in the wilderness without remembering how Sandy always hogged the best sleep-ing bag before we could climb in for the night? He had his own bag, of course, but ours were fluffier. Once on the edge of the Gila wilderness in New Mexico, Lois and I lingered over the campfire coals admiring a full moon. From behind us came an impatient little "woof"—more throat clearing than bark—and we turned to see Sandy pawing at the tent flap, notifying us that, full moon or not, bedtime is bedtime.

How can I ever awaken to a chilly mountain dawn without remembering the time my eager little tentmate at Rocky Mountain National Park awakened me with frantic warnings that something—something *big*—was outside our tent and if I'd let him out, he'd chase it away? He rushed out of the tent ahead of me, followed the scent—and skidded to a halt a few feet from the lead bull of an elk herd. He turned toward me, and the big, brown eyes demanded, "What *are* these things and *why aren't you helping me?*"

How can I ever mow the lawn at St. David's without remembering Sandy snoozing in the shady place beneath the blue spruce? Read in my favorite chair without a loving glance at Sandy in his favorite spot under the brazier? Work in my office upstairs without a reassuring glance at Sandy, sunning himself in the south-facing window of the spare bedroom? Here's his supper dish; there, his brush; here, a supply of the special prescription kidney diet that kept him alive an extra year; there, the bone he hid away under the bed . . .

. . . we gave our hearts to a dog to tear.

Pity the poor cynics who make light of us who anthropomorphize our pets, cremate them, cherish their ashes, grieve at their passing. Let them read Plato and Kipling, Wordsworth, Dickens, Galsworthy, Plutarch, and Pliny the Elder! All of these wrote paeans to their dog friends.

Let the cynic hear Lord Byron's voice singing of the dog:

. . . in life the firmest friend,
The first to welcome, foremost to defend.

Byron's epitaph to his beloved Boatswain could serve equally as ours to Sandy:

Near this spot are deposited the remains of one who possessed beauty without vanity, strength without insolence, courage without ferocity, and all the virtues of Man, without his vices. This praise, which would be unmeaning flattery if inscribed over human ashes, is but a just tribute to the memory of Boatswain, a dog.

Sandy loved and trusted utterly, without reservation. Even as his own powers waned, he never failed to greet Lois at the door after her long, grueling nights at the newspaper office, and the big, brown eyes told her that no deadline-dodging, ego-burdened, self-aggrandizing fauves of the Fourth Estate could drag her down so long as her faithful cocker spaniel drew breath. He was, as Sir Walter Scott put it, given "by the Almighty . . . to be companion of our pleasures and our toils, invested . . . with a nature noble and incapable of deceit."

Of all the dogs of literature, my favorite (and in my mind the most Sandy-like) is John Muir's Stickeen. The great naturalist met the dog on his second trip to Alaska in 1880, and they disliked one another at first; but the animal perversely followed him into the arctic wilds, where Stickeen's incredible bravery throughout a death-defying adventure on a glacier changed man and animal forever. Muir's description of Stickeen's celebration of their delivery from icy death reminds me of Sandy's exuberant behavior on Loveland Pass. Stickeen's "normal fox-like trot" on the trail might also be Sandy's. And well might I write of Sandy, as Muir did of Stickeen:

I have known many dogs, and many a story I could tell of their wisdom and devotion; but to none do I owe so much. . . . Through him as through a window I have ever since been looking with deeper sympathy into all my fellow mortals. He has left this world—crossed the last crevasse—and gone to another. But he will not be forgotten. To me he is immortal.

I knew, and Sandy knew, as we prepared to go west one more time, that he would soon cross the last crevasse. The bright brown eyes that once spoke so eloquently of life and joy and love and trust were clouded now by cataracts; the ears that once heard every wing flutter and distant footfall now sometimes didn't hear his own name when we called it; but each day at fondling time he heard the mantra "Good Sandy! Sandy Good Boy!" and the philosopher's soul glowed bright behind the cataracts, and the eyes said he'd had a rich, full spaniel's life and hadn't it been wonderful?

In those last days on the slick rock shelf on the canyon rim, with the deer passing by every dawn and the eagle circling overhead, with the morning sun sweeping shadow from the canyon floor and warming his arthritic old bones, with the fluffy sleeping bags to be hogged at night, and an Eden of sunny spots and cool shade to bask in, he was at peace.

His eyes wished us well on our day hikes without him and said he knew we understood that he couldn't blaze the trail for us any longer. He was given to long, thoughtful silences staring into nature, having to interrogate it no more, for at last he understood it, as a philosopher must.

And then the day came when the eyes said, "We're there now—the end of the trail, the last crevasse."

Dr. Ken administered a mild tranquilizer, so that Sandy would have no fear, and left us alone with him in a private treatment room to say good-bye. When the final injection was given, he slipped quietly and serenely into his endless sleep.

The last thing he felt was our touch.

The last sounds he heard were our whispered fondnesses. "Good Sandy!" I said. "Sandy Good Boy!"

—Tom Wark

Rocky

I've put off writing this because I know I will cry as I put the memories on paper. Do you ever stop missing the Greatest American Dog in the World?

My older brother gave Rocky to me in 1979 when I was nineteen years old. An unwanted mutt, the dog was on his way to the pound and only six weeks old. He probably could have had a successful career as a celebrity impersonator, because he looked a lot like Benji; however, he was too busy taking care of me to let such mundane pursuits as stardom interfere.

I'll never forget that very first night when he lay in a box by my bed and cried, missing his littermates. I picked him up and cuddled him next to my heart, where he would sleep for the next fifteen years. We soon became inseparable. I found out at Rocky's initial checkup that he had been born with a congenital heart defect that the veterinarian predicted would get worse as Rocky grew. The prognosis was not good, and we left with a two-year life expectancy looming in front of us.

For some reason, I didn't worry about it. I knew that if I loved him enough, he would live forever; and I was almost right. To the amazement of everyone (except Rocky and me, who never had a doubt), his condition remained the same. It never got better, but it never got worse.

Over the years and all the changes of life, Rocky and I were a team. If I cried, he would bring me his toys and kiss me so much that I eventually had no choice but to start laughing and kissing him back. He saw me through a divorce (the result of a "we were way too young to be married" mistake), and through a failed engagement when I was actually stood up on my wedding day! I would have wallpapered my room with "The more I know men the more I love my dog" bumper stickers had I not met the wonderful man with whom I just celebrated ten near-perfect years of marriage, Shawn.

From the beginning of our courtship in 1985, I made it very clear that Rocky and I were a package deal. Shawn never resented Rocky or his place in my life and he became a great daddy. After our marriage in 1986, Rocky kept his rightful place at night, next to my heart, and between Shawn and me!

In 1986, our family grew when we adopted a stray cat,

Cilla. In 1987, we added another stray, Tigger; and in 1989, we adopted Christopher from the animal shelter because he had giant ears and looked like a bat instead of a cat and because it was his last day to be rescued. Rocky adapted well to the new additions, even protecting tiny Christopher from the other cats by walking over him everywhere he went!

In 1993, Rocky was fourteen years old, and Shawn and I were excited to be buying a brand-new home. It was gorgeous; and our down payment was waiting patiently in the bank for close of escrow, when Rocky had heart failure. I rushed him to the vet, who immediately placed him on IVs and put a tube down his throat. She told me that with the right medications and time in the hospital for observation, he could pull through. It was very risky and very expensive, and due to his age, the logical step would be to put him down. I knew that because of the house we were broke. I also knew that Rocky had never given up on me, and I could not give up on him. I called Shawn, and the Greatest Dog in the World proved to me I had the greatest husband in the world.

"Tell the vet to do whatever has to be done to save him. Money is no object," Shawn said. And he continued, "If we have to use our whole down payment we will. We just won't get the house."

I visited Rocky every day in the hospital, and he pulled through. We were still able to get the house, and we settled in.

Rocky was beginning to slow down. He developed cataracts, but could still see well enough to growl from my lap when one of the cats jumped up next to us. He couldn't jump up on the bed anymore, so every night Shawn or I would lift him up so he could take his place between us. He couldn't control his bladder through the night very well, so our new white carpet in the master bath was initiated with yellow, decorative spots. It was okay. How can you value carpet over your best friend?

The Lord blessed us, so I no longer needed to work; and I was with Rocky constantly. When I suffered a miscarriage, he pulled me through. In September 1994, Rocky was fifteen, and a lump on his chest was diagnosed as lymphatic cancer. When the vet said, "Two weeks at most," I remember my knees buckling, and Rocky straining to get out of the vet's arms so he could get to me. Even at his worst hour, he thought only about me. We decided to take him home. He was still eating well and did not appear to have any pain.

From that day on, I never left my house. I realize how crazy this was to most people, but Rocky had never let me go through anything alone, and I would not allow him to be alone when he needed me. If I had to shop or do errands, I waited until my husband got home so he could be with Rocky. I took Rocky over to see my mom and dad, as he had always loved them so much. It was a special time. Two weeks turned into two months, and we got Rocky his first-ever dog Halloween costume so he could run to the door and greet the kids. When Thanksgiving rolled around, Rocky was still sitting up and begging for scraps he was not supposed to have. By December, I began to leave the house for short little trips to the store, and every time I got ready to leave, I would hold Rocky and tell him over and over again, "Wait for Mommy. Don't go anywhere until Mommy gets home." I repeated this mantra for over five minutes; and although I knew Rocky understood, my human friends would roll their eyes and question my sanity.

I began to pray that Rocky would make it through

Christmas; and as the season rolled around, I put his stocking up and took him to the pet store to get his picture taken with Santa. Shawn and I always celebrate on Christmas Eve; so Christmas Eve night Rocky ate his present of prime rib, and we opened his presents for him. The night was perfect, and we had all celebrated one more Christmas together.

Shawn and I always make the hour drive to my parents' for Christmas, and usually Rocky went, but with all the nieces and nephews, we thought it would be too much for him; so I gave him the lecture on waiting for me, as always, and we left.

We were gone longer than planned, the longest I had left Rocky since September. As soon as the garage door began to rise, I began to worry. Usually, Rocky came through the doggie door in the laundry room when he heard the garage and got in the car so he could "ride in" with us. He did not come out, and I ran into the house. I looked at Rocky and he walked up to me, wagging his tail. He put his feet on my leg to be picked up, and I lifted him, looked in his eyes, and told Shawn, "It's time." We sat on the floor, and I held him in my arms, against my heart, as I first had done over fifteen years earlier, trying to comfort him now as I had then.

I started talking to him. I told him how much I loved him and that if his job as a dog was to be loyal and loving and look after me, then he had done the very best job any dog could do. His breathing became shallow, but he kept looking in my eyes; and I realized that, as always, he was worried about me. I choked back the tears and put on a happy voice. I told him, "Rocky, you go ahead and go. Mommy will be okay. When you close your eyes, you'll be able to run fast again and see everything. We'll still be together. We will always be together. Go ahead and go. I'll be okay." He closed his eyes and died in my arms on Christmas night 1994.

The weeks that followed were the worst of my life. All of a sudden, for the first time in fifteen and a quarter years, I was alone. The cats were confused; and Christopher, now five, kept looking for Rocky and crying. Very few people understand the grief involved in losing what to them was "just" a dog but what to you was a *dog*. God's greatest creation and your child; your playmate; your therapist; and above and beyond all else, your very best friend. Rocky enabled me to love everyone and everything around me a little more because of the depth of his love for me, and I know that I could never repay him for all he brought to my life. People always told me Rocky was lucky, but they were wrong. I was the lucky one. I guess in a way I was right fifteen years ago when I thought Rocky would live forever if I just loved him enough. He may no longer be lying next to my heart every night, but he's in my heart night and day, and he will live there forever.

—*Terri L. Collins*

POSTSCRIPT: *As I write this, Austin Collins is lying on my lap asleep. Shawn and I adopted him from the animal shelter two years ago when he was three years old. He is a purebred apricot poodle (about ten pounds), and his tag said he was given away because "there was no time to house-train him." In three years? He learned in a week and never makes a mistake. (I told him even if he does, we value life and love over carpet in this house so don't worry.) Austin is here to stay for as long as God chooses to bless us with him. He is very clingy! He never leaves your lap if you are sitting; and if you are standing, he wants to be held. . . . I guess I'd be clingy too if I*

thought I had a home for three years and ended up look-
ing through bars waiting for my companions to return.
Christopher and Austin chase each other all over the
house; and after Austin was here two weeks, Tigger fi-
nally came out from under the bed! And yes, he sleeps
between us. I had not planned to get another dog, but the
house didn't feel like a home. At first I felt guilty loving
Austin, but I know I wouldn't be capable of loving Aus-
tin so much if Rocky hadn't shown me how. I know my
story is long, but love is hard to condense.

A Gift for Eternity

There was an unlikely family of Mom and Dad, a mongrel cocker bitch named Allie, and a potbellied pig
named Amy. Allie and Amy were a delight to each
other. They played together; they talked to each other;
they slept together. Allie the dog ate pig starter, and
Amy the pig ate dog food.

Then it happened. Amy walked out on the pool cover
one day. The side of the canvas dipped beneath the
water, and Amy slipped under and drowned. When Pat
and Richard Heymann came home from work that
night, in grief and horror they pulled Amy from the
pool, laid her on the deck, and sat beside her, crying.

Allie was five years old, and in all her years, she had a favorite possession, without which she was seldom seen. It was a little green rubber frog. Allie walked over to stand above Amy and, lowering her head, rolled the little green frog out to the pig as a final gift. That night, when Amy was removed for burial, Allie did not take back her frog. It was a gift for eternity.

—Bill Tarrant

CHAPTER TWO

Learning and Growing

All knowledge, the totality of all questions and answers, is contained in the dog.

—Franz Kafka

In his grief over the loss of a dog, a little boy stands for the first time on tiptoe, peering into the rueful morrow of manhood. After this most inconsolable of sorrows there is nothing life can do to him that he will not be able to somehow bear.

—James Thurber

Friday: A Mother's Story

One day, long ago, I was visiting my aunt in Albany, New York. I heard a dog barking insistently and looked out the window and saw a young, enthusiastic ball of energy tied with a rope, about eighteen inches long, to a picnic table. He seemed to be calling out to anyone who would listen, "It's a beautiful day. Is anyone there who will explore the world with me?" I asked my aunt about the dog, and she told me his story. She had often called the humane society because the dog was tied to a short rope all day until his owners would take him in at night directly to the basement. Occasionally, his enthusiasm would allow him to break loose to explore life, and the owners would chase him, throwing rocks at him, to get him back to the picnic table. At that moment, I knew I had to have that dog.

I asked Aunt Virginia to go with me to talk to the owners. I had no idea what I was going to say. When the woman came to the door I heard myself making up a story that my young children were desolate because we had to put our dog to sleep and that their dog looked just like the dog we missed so terribly. Did this woman know if there were any others that looked like their dog? She told me her children had given the dog to her and her husband. They were thinking of getting rid of it. I was shocked, and told her I would be returning home to Massachusetts and would be grateful if I could take the dog with me.

In a half hour she brought the dog to me. He seemed to know that he was starting a new life. He never looked back toward his owners. This beautiful, cream-colored dog of uncertain origin was entrusting his life to me. He was about the size of a German shepherd.

We speculated about his origin and thought he was a mix of Lab and husky. He had never been inside a house before and was bouncing from couch to chair to table and landed on my lap wetting me with kisses saying, "Thank you, thank you. . . . Now, let's go, let's see the world!"

As he settled in next to me on the front seat, with his head on my lap, I said to him, "Your life will never be the same." And it wasn't. Neither was ours. We drove home to Massachusetts, and he seemed to know that he had to be patient for three hours. When we pulled into the driveway he jumped up to get his first glimpse of his new world. He saw a big yard with a stake in the ground attached to a very, very long rope and a run in the backyard that faced onto a large wooded area. He saw three of my four grown children, a black Lab, and a black Norwegian forest cat . . . and he knew that, yes, his life would never be the same! Much excitement followed. He cajoled the Lab, queen of the house and suspect of this young, rambunctious intruder, to play with him. He treed the cat much to his own amazement. "How did I do that?" He ran around, jumping and laughing with us all. Friends came to welcome him to this new world. Occasionally, he would stop, lean against one of us, and cover us with kisses.

What would we name this new member of the family? It was on Friday that he was rescued and on Friday that a new way of life for all of us started. So, it was decided, "Friday" was his name.

When we finally went inside, we discovered he had this incredible ability to jump straight up into the air! If there was something in his path like a coffee table, his exuberance drove him to the most direct route: He would jump straight up over it! If someone was sitting with their legs stretched out, he would jump straight up into the air and over; he was like a kangaroo! We played this game for years and years.

The first morning in his new home, I awoke and went to look for him. I came into the living room and he was sitting on a high table looking out the window. He had never been in a house, he didn't know about furniture. He learned many things in the days that followed. In a short time he learned that it was okay to go downstairs. He wouldn't be locked away, alone in a basement. He was free to come and go. He also learned that a raised hand to his head was no cause to cringe . . . it was a loving touch. Friday and my son Scott formed that special bond between man and dog. Scott spent hours training him to voice commands and to walk with a leash for his own safety. Loyalty and love worked both ways. My belief about loyalty and love is that the more you give, the more you get. I don't know who loved more or who was more loyal, but they both gave all they had and received beyond expectations. Rain, snow, sleet, cold, warm sunshine, day or night, Scott would take Friday to fulfill his dream of exploring life and the world.

He ran free in the woods chasing every movement and every scent. There were deer for him to chase: "Don't run away, I just want to play!" There were squirrels, raccoons, rabbits, and strange rustlings in the underbrush. Such an athlete! Fast as a rocket, leaping straight up into the air to overcome any obstacle in search of new adventure!

His quest for adventure would sometimes overcome his desire to please, and he would not return to voice command. He just couldn't help himself. The gas station would call, "I have Friday here." A stranger on the next street would call, "I have Friday here." The police in the next town would call, "We have Friday here."

The woman with the chicken coop would call, "I have Friday here."

One day I returned from searching by car for Friday in the surrounding area to no avail. I was pacing the living room, and looked out the window as the garbage truck pulled up. There was Friday sitting in the passenger seat! The driver opened the door, and Friday looked back as though to say, "Thanks for the lift!"

He loved the outdoors. When he was lying in the snow for hours, I would worry and want to bring him in. He would say, "No, I am enjoying the fresh snow, dreaming my dreams of the past and the future." I would insist and tug on his rope, he would resist and go limp. He knew best.

How did this gentle giant emerge and survive the oppression of his former life? How did he know to respond to a treat, taking it from our fingers with the slightest touch rather than a bite? How did he respond to our love so readily when he was mistreated in his early life? How did he learn to trust so readily that even when he went to the vet he would jump onto the examining table, believing we all were helping him? What was it that allowed him to be the optimist when his other life taught him nothing but neglect and negativity? I have wondered that for years.

Scott eventually met and married Christina. Scott, Christina, and Friday moved away; and he won the hearts of everyone he met. Christina comes from a big, loving Italian family, and Friday enjoyed freshly grated Parmesan cheese and homemade spaghetti sauce over his food. He became an Italian dog. He loved his extended family and the adventure of new surroundings and new friends. Everyone loved him, young and old. He was about eight or nine years old then, and it was his first encounter with small children. He allowed them to climb and crawl on him with never a complaint. When he tired of them he would come and sit close to Scott, leaning on him as if to say, "Rescue me." Christina's grandmother was eighty-five years old when she died. Her last words to Christina were, "Take care of Friday."

The end of this part of life's adventure came not long ago. He had the best care that love and money could give most of his life, but his athletic body gave out to incurable illness. Even through all his days of hospitalization, he trusted that everyone around him had only the best intentions toward him. When he was given his final injection to give him peace from his illness, he looked to Scott and reached out his paw as though to say, "It's been great, hasn't it? Thanks for the lift!"

Friday leaves behind many things. He leaves a house filled with his warmth and his toys to welcome a new dog rescued from the animal shelter named Tommi, after Christina's grandmother. He leaves a bit of his exuberance and sense of adventure with each of us. He touched us with his indomitable spirit to live and love no matter what happened. His ashes are scattered in the woods in Massachusetts where he loved to run. There he leaves his memory to all living things: "I was here, I lived life every minute, I loved every minute . . . enjoy!" He leaves a legacy of love and laughter. He leaves proof that even when growing up with neglect and oppression it is possible to live and love. After all, the more love and loyalty you give, the more you get.

—*Betty Forbis*
(see "Friday: A Son's Story," p. 271)

Lucky

My boyhood in Brooklyn, some fifty years ago, was surrounded by wonderful parents, brothers, and friends.
Among us humans was Lucky, a Boston terrier, who
seemed to be there forever. Because I was the youngest,
Lucky became my dog. He was playful and very territo-
rial, which makes one memory especially amazing, as I
think back.

I experienced an accident that split my jaw. I had a
big bandage and much discomfort. My mom, to cheer
me up, brought me and my brother to a local movie. It
was near Easter, and they were giving rabbits as a raffle
prize. I got sick and had to go home. I think the movie
manager felt sorry for me because later, here came my
brother carrying home my prize, a cuddly, pink-nosed
rabbit; "Peter," we named him (what else?).

Our glee and excitement quickly halted when we realized not only would we need the approval of Dad, but
what about Lucky? With considerable pleading and
bargaining, Dad agreed to let Peter stay, but eventually,
if they didn't get along, he would have to go.

We put Peter and Lucky together out into the yard,
with much observation and worry. There was the typical smelling and looking at each other with reservation.
A little more each day, it got better and better. There
never was a serious incident. My dad, convinced they
could be pals, built Peter a house in the yard which
Lucky often shared. The rabbit and dog ate together
often. When it got real cold, Dad made an opening into
an extension of the house that allowed Peter to enter.
Although Lucky usually slept near me, it wasn't unusual
to find him in the enclosed area, sleeping near Peter.

One night without warning we had a large snowfall, and Peter was outside. We went out searching for him, but couldn't find him. We were all sure Peter didn't survive the night. But Lucky seemed to know better as he barked continually while we proceeded to dig in the vicinity of Peter's house early the next morning. Suddenly, there was movement—he was alive! Lucky licked him, and we all laughed happily.

The friendship lasted for some time, until Lucky got sick and had to be put down. It wasn't very long until we found Peter gone, lying in his house. We believed Peter died from a broken heart, because his friend had passed away.

They were true buddies, and they were my friends. As I look back now, perhaps they were giving a young boy a message that opposites can get along, especially in a home filled with warmth and love. Not a bad lesson. Thank you, my friends.

—William Crisp

Do You Know What It's Like to Watch Dogs and Children Play?

The story of my two dogs is the reality of the everyday love they bring to my ever-shrinking world. As a workaholic career person, the thought of owning a dog was never considered. Until my world changed and became smaller from a chronic illness.

It was then my husband and I gave in to my son's wishes for a dog. Along came Courtney (black Lab). Eight months later, I gave in to my husband's wishes and along came Crystal (yellow Lab, white shepherd mix). How could I have known what wonders sweet faces and fur can do for pain and loneliness?

At ten months of age, one month after Crystal arrived, Courtney began a series of surgeries on her hips and elbows that would span the next two years. Crystal never left the side of her crate where Courtney recovered.

How could I have known this would teach me to accept myself and others (even dogs) that weren't perfect?

Courtney just turned four last week. She and Crystal are inseparable, as am I with the two of them. Courtney still requires medical followup. Where most dogs would greet the medical community at this point with anger or fear, Courtney greets doctors as though they were friends she had not seen in a while.

How could I have known this would teach me that my illness is not wrath from God or fault of my own? Nothing in nature is perfect, yet nature exists happily despite being imperfect.

My two dogs share the small everyday world of our home with me. They look forward to the evening doorbell ring of the neighbor kids, a signal for them to go out and play. Without my dogs, how could I have known how much I could do in my small world?

Do you know what it's like to watch children and dogs play?

I could stare at the faces of my two dogs all day.

—*Renee Leon*

The Minister's Guru

I am a parish minister by vocation. My work involves the intangible and perhaps undefinable realm of spirit. I pray with the dying and counsel the bereaved. I take part in the joy of parents, christening their newborns and welcoming fresh life into the world. I occasionally help people think through moral quandaries and make ethical decisions, and I also share a responsibility for educating the young, helping them realize their inborn potential for reverence and compassion. Week after week I stand before my congregation and try to talk about the greatest riddles of human existence. In recent years, however, I have become aware that human beings are not the only animals on this planet that participate in affairs of the spirit.

Everyone needs a spiritual guide: a minister, rabbi, counselor, wise friend, or therapist. My own wise friend

is my dog. He has deep knowledge to impart. He makes
friends easily and doesn't hold a grudge. He enjoys simple pleasures and takes each day as it comes. Like a true
Zen master, he eats when he's hungry and sleeps when
he's tired. He's not hung up about sex. Best of all, he
befriends me with an unconditional love that human
beings would do well to imitate.

"I think I could turn and live with the animals,
they're so placid and self-contained," wrote the poet
Walt Whitman. "I stand and look at them long and
long." He goes on:

They do not sweat and whine about their condition,
They do not lie awake in the dark and weep for their
   sins,
They do not make me sick discussing their duty to
   God,
Not one is dissatisfied, not one is demented
   with the mania of owning things,
Not one kneels to another, nor to his kind that
   lived thousands of years ago,
Not one is respectable or unhappy over the whole
   earth.

My dog does have his failings, of course. He's afraid
of firecrackers and hides in the clothes closet whenever
we run the vacuum cleaner, but unlike me he's not
afraid of what people think of him or anxious about his
public image. He barks at the mail carrier and the
newsboy, but in contrast to some people I know he
never growls at the children or barks at his wife.

So my dog is a sort of guru. When I become too
serious and preoccupied, he reminds me of the impor-
tance of frolicking and play. When I get too wrapped
up in abstractions and ideas, he reminds me of the im-

portance of exercising and caring for my body. On his own canine level, he shows me that it might be possible to live without inner conflicts or neuroses; uncomplicated, genuine, and glad to be alive.

Mark Twain remarked long ago that human beings have a lot to learn from the higher animals. Just because they haven't invented static cling, ICBMs, or televangelists doesn't mean they aren't spiritually evolved.

No one can prove that animals have souls. But if we open our hearts to other creatures and allow ourselves to sympathize with their joys and struggles, we find they have the power to touch and transform us. There is an inwardness in other creatures that awakens what is innermost in ourselves.

For ages people have known that animals have a balance and harmony we can learn from. "Ask the beasts, and they will teach you," counsels the Book of Job. Other creatures have inhabited the earth much longer than we have. Their instincts and adaptations to life are sometimes healthier than our own. "In the beginning of all things," said the Pawnee Chief Letakots-Lesa, "wisdom and knowledge were with the animals; for Tirawa, the One Above, did not speak directly to man. He sent certain animals to tell me that he showed himself through the beasts, and that from them, and from the stars and the sun and the moon, man should learn." The concept that other living beings can be our spiritual guides is really nothing new.

With love and affection, then, I dedicate these thoughts to the animals of the world, but especially my own spiritual guide. Other people have their mentors, masters, and teachers. I have a doggone mutt.

—*Gary Kowalski*

Chip

In August 1975, my mother decided it would be all right for me to have a puppy from the next-door neighbor's brand-new litter. The puppies were a mix of beagle and pointer—unique and very beautiful. The puppy I chose had a beautiful white coat with a brown patch on top of her head shaped exactly like a heart. I felt an instant connection with her because I had a heart-shaped birthmark on my shoulder.

At this time I was four years old and my father had just died of cancer. Having a new puppy around the house was a godsend for me, as my mother was an emotional wreck and could not give me the support I needed. I fell in love immediately with my new dog and gave her the name Chip.

I often think I would have withdrawn into my own closed world, hidden away from everyone, if it hadn't been for my dog. I never seemed to get along with others very well as a child, and it didn't take long for Chip to become my best and only friend. She would sit in my lap; we would listen to the radio, go for walks, run, and play. I would tell her all my troubles and concerns. She would sleep under the covers with me at night so I wouldn't be scared—it was almost as if she were the sibling I never had. We grew very close and shared our lives together.

By the time I was nine, my mother had been through three marriages. I suffered many emotional setbacks at a very tender age. I became more and more dependent on myself and distrustful of others. I was excessively shy, had a terrible self-image, and hated going to school. I was often teased about my height, and I was continuing to sprout up quickly for my age.

The only one I could ever count on was Chip. I was the center of her universe. She accepted me no matter what I did or what I looked like. Animals have taught me such a wonderful lesson. They know no prejudice or hatred. We call them "dumb" for this childlike innocence, but I think they are blessed.

As the years rolled along, I started to change, to grow up. Eventually my height wasn't laughed at anymore, but envied instead. Through all those years of keeping to myself, I had become a good artist, poet, and musician; but most important, I learned to be very sensitive to the feelings of others. I learned patience, understanding, and caring.

I owe this all to my dog, Chip, because she was the one in my life who showed me all of these things. No human ever taught me these concepts—she's the only one I can thank. With her help, I can finally say that I am happy with who I am. I made it through a type of childhood that all too often leads to drug and alcohol abuse. I don't know that I could say that if I had been completely alone back then.

Three years ago, I met a man who showed me kindness and caring that I have never known from another person. I knew from the beginning that he would stay with me and take care of me forever. I also knew that my emotional problems would be a major obstacle to overcome, but with his support and love I have torn down many of my walls.

One night in February 1993, my dog lay down for the last time and refused to eat or drink. I knew in my heart it was time for her to go. I tried not to be bitter; eighteen years is a long time to have a dog. But because of the role she played in my life, I could not help but feel that part of me was dying, too.

I held Chip close all night long as tears streamed

down my face and thousands of memories played over and over in my head. I think she somehow knew there was someone here who would be watching out for me and taking care of me from now on. She had stayed with me for as long as I needed her, but I was no longer a lonely child in need of love, and she was very old and tired.

As the night wore on, we listened to the radio, and a song played that we had often heard eighteen years before. The song was about two best friends and the pain they feel when one of them discovers he is dying. I never paid much attention to the lyrics as a child, but the words were now piercing my heart. The next morning, Valentine's Day, my beautiful friend died in my arms.

The once heart-shaped fur on her head was now mostly gray and didn't much resemble a heart at all. I thought back to the time when she was a roly-poly baby, brand-new and full of life. I could not believe this was the same dog, so lifeless in my arms. Those childhood days suddenly seemed like a different lifetime.

Not a day goes by that I don't think of Chip and miss her. I thank God every day for giving me such a wonderful gift. He knew I needed her, and He sent her to grow up with me.

I have always been told that animals don't go to heaven, but if God ever makes any exceptions, I know Chip will be there.

—Kimberlee L. Lippencott

Heidi

She was a gift from my grandmother to my sister and me. We went to a small house with a large yard to pick Heidi out from a litter of schnoodles (schnauzer/poodle mix). Of all of her brothers and sisters, she seemed to be the smartest and cutest. She had beautiful dark hair, and she was only five weeks old. She was the smallest, most adorable puppy I had ever seen . . . and I loved her from the moment I saw her.

Heidi stayed in the kitchen, where newspapers were spread across the floor, in a cardboard box turned onto its side, until she was big enough to know how and when to let us know that she had to go outside. It didn't take long, though. She was smart from the start. Once we gave her the run of the house, she soon learned to jump up at the front door, as if she were trying to turn the knob herself, when she wanted to go out in her fenced-in side yard. That was the first thing she learned. That and the fact that the side yard was hers, and hers alone. The gate never closed on that small fenced-in area because she was smart enough to go straight to her yard, do her business, and come straight back to the front door where she waited ever so patiently until we remembered to let her in.

Next, she learned the standard tricks; roll over, sit, stand, stay. We could put a cookie on her nose, and she wouldn't even blink until we said *okay*. She would roll on her back and play dead whenever anyone pointed their finger at her and yelled "Bang!" The neighbors used to love watching her run down to the end of the driveway every single morning to fetch the paper and bring it right to the front door, where my mother would give Heidi her morning cookie. And when the paperboy would accidentally throw the paper under a bush, or in some tall grass, no worry, Heidi would simply grab the neighbor's paper for us. She was so clever, and the most intelligent animal I've ever owned.

Shortly after her third birthday she started to get sick. I don't remember exactly what the first signs were, but they were enough to indicate that we had to take her to the vet. We were informed that our dog had diabetes. She would require two shots of insulin every day for the rest of her life if she was going to live. My parents had tossed around the idea of having her put to sleep, and even I had thought that it may have been best that way. But eventually we decided that we could not do that to her. Not after all the joy she had brought us. Not after all she had done for us, could we take away her life just because she would require more of us. We decided that she would live, and we would do everything possible to keep her alive.

Well, after months of experimenting with different amounts of food and levels of insulin, we came to a happy medium that allowed Heidi to live a normal dog life. She actually looked forward to getting the shots of insulin, because she knew she would get a cookie afterward. She rarely flinched, and she often took the shots better than most humans I know.

Heidi lived six more years after being diagnosed with diabetes, for a total of nine glorious years. Toward the end, though, things got rough. She developed cataracts and had to have one of her eyes removed, which was another time when we had pondered whether or not it would be best for Heidi to put her to sleep. Once again, we decided that we could all get through this. She also developed tumors under the skin, and at this point we began to wonder how much longer she could hold on. She looked old. The stitched-up eye socket, the lumps on her body, the milky haze in her remaining eye. It was sad to look at her, but the love we all felt for her was so strong.

She passed away one day while no one was home. My mother and sister came home to an empty house, Heidi was nowhere to be found. They searched everywhere until they found her, in the far corner of the basement, next to the furnace. My mother called me at work and I rushed home. I was in tears the whole way. When I came home, Heidi was in her bed with a blanket covering her and all of her toys around her. We all began to cry. We put her to rest, and tried to move on. But she will always be in our hearts.

My mother still reminds us that the medical bills that the dog rang up were extraordinary, but she loved Heidi just as much as we did. Heidi taught us a lot about life. She taught us responsibility. She taught us that some things are worth the trouble. She taught us that life is the most precious gift on earth and that even when you are totally dependent, you still have the ability to change someone's life forever.

We miss you, Heidi. You are in our hearts forever.

—Steven Buck

CHAPTER THREE

Loyalty and Friendship

His name is not Wild Dog anymore, but First Friend, because he will be our friend for always and always and always.

—Rudyard Kipling

My boxer Gangster is the truest friend I can ever ask for.

—Sylvester Stallone

Faithful Dog Hachiko

Between the world wars, in Tokyo's Shibuya section, there lived a golden-brown Akita dog named Hachiko. The famous tale of her loyalty and devotion to her master is so familiar in Tokyo that she is universally known as "*chu-ken* Hachiko," or "faithful dog Hachiko."

Hachiko, born in 1922, was the pet of Professor Eisaburo Ueno of Tokyo University. Ueno lived in Shibuya, then considered a suburb but now a very trendy Tokyo neighborhood. Every morning, the professor would walk from his home to Shibuya Station to take the train to work—and every morning Hachiko came with him.

Each afternoon, when Ueno came back home on the afternoon train, Hachiko would be waiting on the platform to meet him. All the other commuters and the merchants of Shibuya came to know and love the dog and await her daily vigil.

One day in 1925, Ueno died suddenly while at work. Faithful Hachiko waited and waited at the station that night, but her master did not come home.

So Hachiko came back to wait for her master again the next afternoon. And the next, and the next. In fact, she kept coming back to the station, through rain, snow, and the occasional earthquake, every afternoon for the next ten years.

Hachiko died in 1935 but her utter devotion and love live on. Shibuya Station, at the Hachiko statue, is where lovers meet.

To avoid lovers' quarrels, the Japanese have placed, at Hachiko's statue, a machine that lets you punch in on arrival and issues a card saying what time you arrived.

Thus lovers can prove to each other that they arrived

at Shibuya Station right on time—just as faithful dog Hachiko did for all those lonely years.

—*T. R. Reid*

Ashlee

If you can imagine a dog that looks like a water buffalo in the water and a black bear out of the water—you have my Ashlee.

I have attempted several times this week to write something about Ashlee. I wanted to share what I think is a wonderful story about a true companion animal, a wonderful friend, and someone I will never forget. I truly miss her with all my heart, and sometimes the wonderful memories of her come flooding back.

I do the best I can, but even after all this time the pain of losing my dearest friend is so great that I still cry uncontrollably and have to leave the room, being unable to function at my desk and sobbing so hard it takes my breath away.

There is a quote by Konrad Lorenz: "The fidelity of a dog is a precious gift demanding no less binding moral responsibilities than the friendship of a human being. The bond with a true dog is as lasting as the ties of this earth can ever be." I truly believe this. I am so lucky to have had my relationship with Ashlee.

My daughter had just started a clerical job at a wholesale tobacco and candy warehouse. She and a friend were on their way to Ocean City, Maryland, for Labor Day weekend when she found two tiny puppies on the roadside. One was a little black fuzz ball and the other was kind of a brindle. They were approximately nine weeks old. My daughter turned around to come home, canceling her trip to the beach, and walked in the house with these two puppies. We already had a dog, a ten-year-old who had been ailing for some time, and I really did not want another. She told me not to worry, she was going to find homes for them. She did find a home for the brindle immediately, but didn't seem too anxious to find the black one a home.

My daughter left home for several days under the pretext that she was looking for a home for the black puppy. When she returned, I was not home, so she left me a note on the kitchen counter telling me she had come home to pick up some things, and the puppy was in her room with the door closed and not to touch it. I thought for a moment and said out loud, "What does she mean, don't touch it?" Well, needless to say, my daughter knew exactly what she was doing, as I went into her room and picked up the puppy; we immediately became bonded for life. My daughter was so smug but also upset as she thought the puppy would be hers, but it was obvious this was going to be my friend for life.

My other dog became paralyzed and had to be put to sleep, which caused my newfound friend to become even closer to me. My vet examined the new puppy and guessed at her age; we also guessed that she was a black Lab/Australian shepherd cross, whom my daughter named Ashlee. The vet also felt that in her ordeal on the highway, she may have been hit by a car or dropped from a very high place as she had a severe hip malfunction or displacement. It didn't seem to hamper her in any way, so we decided not to treat it at that time.

Over the years, Ashlee went everywhere with me (except to work). She was a constant companion. She was a wonderful traveler, and she helped me scribe at horse shows. She went trail riding with me and supervised all the other pets at the barn. We communicated all the time, Ashlee with her ears and eyes, the tilt of her head, and the wag of her little nub of a tail. I was constantly talking to her. She would tell me when the cats had gotten into the closet and I had unknowingly shut the door on them. Ashlee knew they were in there and would come tell me. She would tell me the phone was ringing if I was in the back of the house. She would tell me the washer had become unbalanced—she was so smart.

I retired early from a major computer company in 1990. Ashlee and I set out to do what we loved best— being together. The first year was the most fun and the happiest I had ever been in my entire life. Ashlee and I did a lot of house sitting/farm sitting for local people. We enjoyed every day together at work or play. Some of the people I farm-sat for had in-ground swimming pools. Ashlee and I had a wonderful time swimming and lying around the pool. Ashlee did most of the lying around. She loved the second step into the pool. She looked like a musk ox or a water buffalo. She would sort of float in the front, take a mouthful of water, and then let it spout out from each side of her mouth. But she loved it when I went off the diving board. She would run around to the opposite side of the pool and jump in, swimming to me, taking my wrist in her mouth and rescuing me. Even though I was standing up, I would pretend that she was saving me and make such a fuss over her. I loved her so much.

When we would go trail riding, her favorite thing to do was to go swimming in the creek. I would let my horse stand in the creek on a long rein and Ashlee would take pleasure in just paddling around, swimming, and being a water buffalo.

In May or June 1991 we relocated to another horse farm. However, I wasn't as active as I had been. I seemed to be drained of energy. I tried helping out the owners of the new farm as much as possible. In late September or very early October I started not feeling well. The doctor couldn't find anything. Ashlee seemed to sense something was not quite right. She followed me more and more, not letting me out of her field of vision. If I rode in the outdoor arena, she needed to be where she could see me. If I rode indoors, she would stay in the doorway or behind the mounting block, out of harm's way.

However, in 1991 I was outside with Ashlee, and I didn't feel good. I thought I had the flu or indigestion and I asked a neighbor who was a nurse if she would check my respiration and temperature. She did and then suggested that we call an ambulance. I was having a heart attack. I was taken to a local hospital, which did not have the necessary cardiology unit to perform the angioplasty that I had to have on three arteries. After the surgery, they brought me back to the local hospital to intensive care and then to the coronary care unit.

The fleeing ambulance was the last thing Ashlee saw as I went off to the hospital. She stood silently at the lamppost where the ambulance had been and did not want to go back into the house. My daughter and a neighbor had to force her. Once inside, she was despondent—she wouldn't eat, drink, or go out. My daughter would carry her down the step and take her out, but she would just sit under the street lamp and sulk. The nurse in the hospital heard my daughter and me talking about it, and she suggested to my daughter that after the administrative personnel left the hospital for the day, she bring Ashlee down so that she could see that I was all right.

My daughter was nervous—she didn't want to be caught by hospital administration personnel smuggling this dog into my room. But Ashlee was not the slightest bit apprehensive about getting into the elevator. She even seemed excited and walked down the hallway quite briskly to my room. When Ashlee entered my room, she apparently picked up my scent and came over to my bed. I got out of the bed, and sat down on the floor, IV and all. She had a way of wagging her little nub that wagged her entire body. We both cried, and she took her paw and forearm and wrapped it around my arm, she rolled over on her side, and I just hugged this eighty-pound dog and cried and cried. I was never so happy to see anyone in my life—and she me. She kissed me and I kissed her. The nurses were all in tears. We didn't have much time as we didn't want to put the nursing staff that allowed her to come to the hospital in an awkward position. I was on a heart monitor, but when it was time for them to leave, I wanted to go down to the parking lot with them. I decided to go down with them, rolling my IV along with me. When I put Ashlee into my daughter's car, she was sad to leave me again but seemed to understand. When I got back to my room, the nurses were all in a panic as I had not told them what I was doing, and my heart monitor had gone off the machine—flatlined—and they couldn't find me. I was so happy, I didn't care that I was in trouble.

After Ashlee returned home, secure in the knowledge that I was fine, she was fine, too. She started eating, going out, and returning to normal. Still, when she went outside she stood by the lamppost.

When I came home she greeted me with great excitement and enthusiasm and then gave me the cold shoulder for the next few days. I could feel that my absence had hurt her.

In 1994 she was diagnosed with so many unhealthy things and had one hip completely gone. The vet felt it did not make any sense to have her go through surgery for her hip and take the chance she would not pull through.

In January 1995 I adopted another dog to keep her company and to help me through what I knew in my heart was going to happen soon. On August 14, 1995, she was so crippled, barely able to walk; she was having kidney problems and eating disorders and so much more. We went down to take our stroll, the last stroll of the evening. I carried her down the stairs and outside. She did not want to go with us—I knew it was time. She told me with her eyes. I loved her too much to not know what she was saying to me. I slept on the floor with Ashlee all night before taking her to the vet the next morning.

I can only hope that one day we will be together again.

—*Barbara DeMambro*

The Kitten

Our beloved dog Teddy had lost his battle with old age, leaving behind Toby, our eight-year-old bichon; Domino, our eighteen-year-old cat who spent most of her time sleeping; my daughter, Wendi; and me, filled with grief. Then Wendi came up with the idea that we should get Toby a kitten, for companionship. He always liked cats, and I wasn't prepared to bring another dog into the house. He had been Teddy's shadow all of his life and was, undoubtedly, in a state of painful confusion.

So we took Toby, and off to the local animal shelter we went. We decided that we should let Toby pick his own kitten.

I guess Wendi and I had an instinctive feeling, because we never questioned the concept, and the caretaker at the shelter agreed to let us take Toby into the cat room.

Wendi held Toby, and I went to the first cage, picking out a fluffy little gray thing, and held it up to Toby. He actually recoiled. I selected another ball of fur, but he was clearly disinterested. Finally, I came to a tiny orange kitten and Toby came to life. He started making noises and tried to lick this poor frightened baby, who was wiggling and crying. We could hardly believe what we were seeing. I went through the routine again, holding up one kitten after another. Once again, when I brought out the orange one Toby nearly jumped out of Wendi's arms. We let him lick her, and it was clear that she was the one. Even the guard couldn't believe what she had witnessed. It was so clear that Toby had made a choice.

What is even more remarkable is what happened

when we got home with our new kitten. We let her out of the box, and she immediately ran to Toby. He started licking her and she cuddled up to him. She wouldn't let me or my daughter touch her for at least a week. She would cry every time we would try to pick her up. But she followed Toby everywhere. He groomed her and she nursed on him. He nudged her around the house, as if he were showing her around. She slept next to him and purred.

As time went on she became more playful and would tease him, pulling at his tail or his collar. He never minded. He would lie right on top of her and snuggle and she would just lie there and purr. This relationship is the most beautiful love between species.

What is so strange is how it seems as if these two knew each other. Like they were old friends. I really don't have an explanation. I just know what I've witnessed.

Tulip is now four years old, and she and Toby continue their special bond. They still play and tease. Sometimes when I wake up in the morning they will both be on my bed. Tulip will be stretched out, purring, while Toby cleans her ears.

—Barbara Brighton

Puppy Love

Milos Forman, the Academy Award–winning director of *One Flew over the Cuckoo's Nest, Amadeus, Ragtime*, and *Hair*, was in Memphis filming a movie when he experienced love at first sight—and adopted a bloodhound puppy. The director named the dog Woody Chrudos, and the pup was his constant companion throughout the remainder of the filming of *The People vs. Larry Flynt*.

"My most touching moment during filming in Memphis was when we were shooting in a small town outside of Memphis at a prison," Forman remembered. "The puppy was several weeks old, and he slept most of the time, so we never left him alone. So, for example, when we went out to a restaurant, the puppy went with us and sometimes slept in the car outside, with all of us taking turns to get up and go check on him every few minutes.

"One day we were going to a restaurant on one of the main streets where you can't park. The nearest parking lot was like five hundred yards away. Standing there, suddenly I see this policeman. I said, 'Listen, can you tell me if there is any other parking place close by? We have to go every few minutes and check on this puppy.' "

Forman insists the police officer did not know he was talking to a world-renowned filmmaker—and the director didn't volunteer the information.

"I am sure of that," Forman said. "We were driving some kind of a plain car, a Ford or something, so I am absolutely sure he did not know who I was. So I was very, very surprised when he said, 'Well, put the car on the sidewalk here, and I'll check it.' "

Forman laughed as he recalled the story. "So we put the car on the sidewalk in front of the restaurant. We were eating, and soon one of us went out to check on the puppy. And there we see this policeman standing there—right beside the car, guarding it. He is waving and smiling and shouts over to reassure us, 'It's okay— the puppy is still sleeping. Everything's okay.'

"I mean, can you imagine this. It was just unbelievable. I was so touched."

—*Linda Romine*

First the Dog

In November 1957, Laika, a random-bred dog of middle size, became the first living earth-creature to travel into space. Photographs of her smiling face in its helmetlike harness and of the network of wires that tracked her responses appeared in newspapers around the world, and millions of well-wishers followed her journey in *Sputnik 2* (or, as Ed Herlihy of *Movietone News* archly dubbed it, *Muttnik*). It was soon clear, however, that she would not return. She barked; floated weightless in space; ate food from a dispenser; and after a week, when the air in the cabin ran out, she died.

In a moving poem dedicated to Laika, "First the

Dog," the distinguished Polish poet Zbigniew Herbert
wrote:

so first the dog honest mongrel
which has never abandoned us
dreaming of earthly lamps and bones
will fall asleep in its whirling kennel
its warm blood boiling drying away

but we behind the dog and second
dog which guides us on a leash
we with our astronauts' white cane
awkwardly we bump into stars
we see nothing we hear nothing

—*Marjorie Garber*

Popeye

Been gone for a long time, never forgotten. He was a
good ol' boy, born somewhere in the Blue Ridge
Mountains. Endured a lot of hard times with us, and
the good times, too. The old man got him when he was
just a tiny pup and Pop hung tough for damn near
seventeen years. In the end I reckon he just got tired.
Deaf, gimpy with arthritis, shotgun pellets in his ass,

shrapnel wounds perhaps from taking down a deer (or a prize cow) or from messing around with the wrong woman. But Popeye was always one hell of a dog. Scare the life out of an intruder (or mailmen or cops), alls we had to do was just grab that ruff of fur around his neck and holler "Go!" Climb a six-foot fence, ford a raving river for a stick or a Frisbee. Didn't have much tolerance for other male dogs or cats of any kind. Nope, none a'tall. Had a few war wounds to prove it, too.

Pop used to run away. Not because he didn't love us. Just because. Doggie wanderlust and a crazy need for adventure. The old man always ran ads in the paper for him (sure, Pop could read) or just mapped out miles and scrounged around till he found Pop. One time these kids had him tied to a tree, had renamed him Killer and were counting on siccing him on other dogs. Another time, some old redneck had him and was going to breed him with his dog, that's just how good-looking Popeye was. I suppose the only time Pop didn't want to come back home was the time he ran off and landed on easy street. Be damned if some rich one wasn't riding Pop around on his yacht, feeding him top sirloin and calling him "Handsome." But the old man whistled and Pop sailed right on up into the bed of that pickup truck. Think he held a grudge about being found that time.

Popeye crossed the country at least three times and back, in all sorts of bogus vehicles—slept in motels and under trucks and out in the cold and down by the river. He was always there and he was always just a good ol' boy. He's buried up in the Oregon Cascades next to a river, in the cool of an old Douglas fir. He died in California, but the old man didn't feel it was fitting to lay his boy down in the land o' fruit and nuts. So, we made a sad sojourn to lay Pop away fittin'. The old man got drunk and stayed drunk for about a year after Pop died. The old man won't ever be the same. I'm just glad he didn't have Pop stuffed and mounted on wheels so he could always have him nearby. Took a heap of talking, but I finally convinced the old man that Pop was the best of dogs and deserved a safe, comfortable place to rest.

So, Popeye, here's to you, boy. Thanks for being a fine friend and courageous companion.

Stout of heart, Sound of spirit
the very last of all the Carolina Yeller Dogs
Good Boy.
Popeye The Dog

> —*Anonymous from the Virtual Pet Cemetery*

Fala

As told to *The Washington Post* upon the unveiling of the FDR memorial with the bronze likeness of Fala in Washington, D.C.

EDITORS' NOTE: FDR died in the spring of 1945. "When General Eisenhower came to Hyde Park to lay a wreath on Roosevelt's grave," wrote historian Doris Kearns Goodwin, "Fala heard the sirens of the motorcade and thought his master was returning. His ears pricked up, Eleanor noted." Fala lost his spirit after FDR died and lived less than five years afterward. He was buried near FDR's grave in Hyde Park.

My late husband, Felix Belair, Jr., was a White House reporter for *The New York Times*. One day, he came home and announced, "Pack your bags, we're going to Miami." [Franklin Delano] Roosevelt was going fishing for two weeks and reporters could bring their wives. We traveled on a train, and it took three days because of Roosevelt's little dog, Fala. Every two to three hours, the train would stop, and someone would get off to walk Fala. We never saw the president getting on, or off, the train, but we did see a lot of Fala on that trip.

—Margaret Belair

Dog and God

Brownie was my first dog when I was a kid, a great collie-shepherd cross. He never allowed anyone to fight and came to my defense when I was getting beaten up by my brothers. He lived to be sixteen and was eventually not able to get around as well as he used to. My dad and mom said he had to go to the hospital. I asked, Will he come back? And they said they did not know. My dad, a truck driver with a great big heart, had to take him to the vet's. Brownie never came home. My dad was really upset, as he told us Brownie had died in his arms at the vet's. I never saw my dad cry except at a funeral of a loved one. But right then and there I knew how much Brownie meant to him. In fact, forty-four years later I still have his collar, as my dad could never throw it away.

Tag Along came to me on my tenth birthday. He was a toy fox terrier, looked a great deal like Wishbone the TV dog. He was a very smart fellow. He could understand sign language, Italian, German, and of course English. My mother was diagnosed with cancer, and Tag stayed by her side all the time. During her last year on earth, she was bedridden, and we did everything to help her. Tag was always there for her. When she had to go to the hospital he went along, and we sneaked him up to help keep Mom happy. A couple of times the nurses and doctors caught us and gave us grief, but we ignored them and brought him again and again. When she passed away, Tag was a few miles from the hospital, but he knew she had gone. He would not stop crying for a week.

After the spring thaw we went to find her grave; the tombstone had not been set yet, but Tag found her instantly. He lived to be eighteen years old and fathered several pups, even in his old age. He was one of the greatest friends of my early life.

Many people say dogs are dumb. Right! How come a dog understands us when we are happy, low, serious? How can they understand our language and we cannot comprehend theirs?

God gave mankind dogs to watch over us, so that no matter what we do, the noble dog is always at our side.

Native Americans tell the story that when Mother Earth was breaking up, all the animals jumped to one side and man stood on the other side. As the earth split open, only one animal jumped to the side of man—yes, the dog. Spell dog backward and you spell *god*.

Baron Hans, our St. Bernard, started to go downhill in the fall of 1995. His hips went out and we had to help him, carry him and all. I could not bear putting him down. The vet said he was not in pain, and we tried every medicine on the block and then some. He would rally, but the times were hard. I was working on the road, opening up casinos, and on April 8, 1996, he passed away at the vet's with my brother, Al, holding him. I was opening the Stratosphere casino in Vegas, and was teaching employees when he passed away. I still have not properly grieved for him.

Hans loved puppies, just like all the other great gals and guys we've owned and cherished, and it is my sincere belief he stayed alive this long to help them. Picture a 180-pound St. Bernard, thirty-six-inch collar, playing with a ball of fluff that was maybe eight ounces tops! Pups would pull on his ears and tail and walk all over him, and he never was nasty. When we could not find a pup or two we'd call him and there they were under his chin. He was a gentle and noble giant.

We spend more money on our dogs than we do on ourselves, and I could not think of any better way. People think we are strange; we aren't. We are normal people. We love and cherish dogs and, yes, cats too.

To all of my friends who have gone before me, I know you are with God and I only pray one day, soon, I will join you and we can all play again.

God bless you all with all our love.

—*Tom and Al Ambrosia*

chose a restaurant, at which point she curled up a discreet distance away from our table and went to sleep. "She must want food," somebody said, and we threw her a piece of bread that she didn't seem to notice. What she did notice, however, was other dogs. Sweetie growled fiercely at any dog brave enough to come near us, making sure we (and that curious dog) knew we had a protector as well as a companion. No matter what we did to dissuade her, Sweetie walked with us back to our condo, curled up in the middle of the road, and went to sleep. "She must belong to someone," said Roz, "because she's wearing a fresh flea collar. Somebody loves her." Diane got up several times during the night and checked the road. The dog remained curled up there, guarding us until morning, when she disappeared.

Clearly a cross between a black Lab and a German short-haired pointer: legs white from foot to knee, lots of black and white spots, black head, black body, long tail, soft gentle eyes. Sweetie became the subject of our conversation all that next day. "Maybe some tourists drove here with their dog and left it here. She must have been *somebody's* dog!" On the other hand, we reasoned, a Labrador might have been left by an American tourist and gotten involved with a dog brought by a German tourist. Didn't see her until we were on our way back from dinner that evening, but this time she was curled up under the table of a young German couple who were as surprised by her attentions as we had been the previous night ("Ve haf not a dog in Dusseldorf"). Roz went over to Sweetie, who got up happily, wagged her tail mightily, put one paw up on Roz's knee, and licked her with great pleasure. To our vast relief, Sweetie stayed with her new friends and didn't follow us home. Next night, however, she was waiting at the place where we first spotted her, followed us to dinner, curled up in the place nearest our table and least inconvenient for the restaurant, and after dinner continued to guard us overnight. Like it or not, we now had a dog.

The last night of our trip Sweetie was waiting for us at the entranceway of the Xaman-Ha Condominiums. As the dog acknowledged us, a couple we'd never met called out, "Look! There's Socks! Hi, Socks!" The dog looked at them for a moment, seemed to nod, and then turned back to us. "You know this dog?" I asked.

In a clear midwestern accent, the wife answered, "The owners of our condo unit keep a guest book so everyone who stays there can say hello. I think they're from the Northwest Territories of Canada, so we kind of know their weather. But a few people have left messages in the book about Socks, saying that she is a real sweetie, and that we should take care of her if we see her. But this is the first time we've seen her." Another tourist couple was walking down the road, called out, "Hi, Socks!" and gave me the same story of messages about the dog left in the guest book of their unit.

The mystery was solved by yet another woman standing among us, and the rest of the story is really hers. Von Ann Stutler ("Von is Dutch. Yvonne without the Y," she said) is a musical contractor who, with her husband and their partner (a homeowner in Playacar), own and operate the Westchester Broadway Theater in Elmsford, New York. She's the kind of sober, thoughtful woman with whom anybody, anywhere would strike up a conversation. "I've been coming here for several years. We really love Playa del Carmen. Everybody knows Socks. She's had at least two litters we know about—the boys at Señor Frog's [bar-restaurant] took care of her with the last litter, maybe eight puppies. All of the black-and-white dogs in Playacar are her children.

"A couple of years ago my friend Julie and I couldn't stand seeing her go into heat all the time, and we didn't think she could handle another pregnancy. Socks was thin and listless, not her usual peppy self. This is a dog who loves to romp in the surf and walk and run with everyone. So we took her to the vet to get spayed. What we didn't know was that spaying is done differently in Mexico. To save time and money he removed only her uterus, leaving the ovaries, so she continued to go into heat and whenever she did, she was chased by all the male dogs in the neighborhood. Thank God that vet left the area, and we got a new one. Once Socks got vaginitis so severe that none of the antibiotics the vet used would work, and he insisted on putting her to sleep because there was nothing he could do to end her suffering. But even after he gave her the lethal injection Socks survived. She simply wouldn't die. So the vet laughed, saying 'I guess she was meant to live,' and within a day or so after he tried to euthanize her, Socks pulled through and the infection was over. A few months later a new vet came to town and he agreed to remove her ovaries so she finally could live more comfortably. We think she's eight or nine.

"The locals are really strange about dogs. Many kids are given a puppy for their birthday, but after a dog grows up no one wants to take care of it, and it is released into the jungle or allowed to run free in town. Then it becomes part of the pack that wanders around a town scrambling for scraps. Even worse, kids are raised by their grandmothers, who threaten them by saying, 'If you're not good I'll throw you to the dogs.' The restaurant guys hate the dogs and often put out poisoned food for them. Socks had a best friend, Pedro, a beautiful brown male who used to pal around with her, and one of the restaurants gave them poisoned food. Socks didn't take any, but Pedro did and got terribly sick. Socks dragged her friend over a mile to my house, but I was away for a couple of days. Then she dragged the dog to another friend of mine, barking until she woke up that house. By the time my friend realized it was Socks and tried to take care of Pedro, it was too late. You may have noticed that she's limping a bit tonight. One of the restaurant guys must have kicked her today."

Von Ann was right about the local folk and their pets. In one shop we met a saleswoman who was proud to show us her pets—an iguana that cuddled and a boa constrictor that played necktie—but considered ownership of a dog unthinkable.

"Both the Mexican and the American homeowners in Playacar were very concerned about how badly the dogs are treated in Playa del Carmen. We're friendly with Jerry Van Dyke [star of the televison show *Coach*], who's got a house on the beach here. Jerry and others in Playacar have tried to educate people about how to take care of dogs, trying to teach a new kind of responsibility. We have a new vet and a clinic now, and they neuter as many dogs as possible to control the population. The animals also receive basic vaccines, such as rabies and distemper, paid for by donations. Jerry entertained at a dinner to raise money to provide the necessary services, and a lot of folks have come forward to help. Next month I'm giving a course in dog grooming to a bunch of locals. If they can turn it into a little business, maybe people will take enough pride in their dogs to take better care of them. It's a long-term project, but we're doing well."

Every time Von Ann comes to Playacar she brings

Socks a new flea collar, and for the period of time the Stutlers are in town, Socks is fed the best canned dog food Von Ann can bring in from the States. That, and her bad experiences taking food from people she can't trust, explains why Socks refused the food we offered her that first night. "But why," I asked, "does she bother to go into Playa del Carmen when you're here? Why doesn't she just stay near your house?" Von Ann smiled and said quietly, "That's who she is. She knows I'm not here all the time. Her life is attaching to people. It's the way she's survived."

I glanced back and forth between Sweetie/Socks and Von Ann Stutler. Sweetie was ready to leave with us for a night on the town. I turned to Von Ann and said, "Call her. She's your dog, not ours. It's only fair that you have fun with her."

"I'll try," she said, "but watch what happens." Von Ann called the dog whose life she had saved on so many occasions, but Socks stayed put, ready to walk with us. Roz and Von Ann exchanged dog-lover looks and smiled.

"C'mon, Sweetie," said my wife happily. "Let's go to dinner." That night, after dinner, Socks gave each of us—Alan, Diane, Roz, and me—a farewell lick, but remained in the town of Playa del Carmen rather than accompany us to the condo in Playacar.

We'll go back to the Xaman-Ha Condominiums next year, and probably for as many years as that particular resort community remains as friendly and funky as it is right now. But if you go, and I hope you do, check in with Socks for us. Just say "Hello, Sweetie" when you see her and you'll enjoy the companionship of one of the smartest dogs we've ever met.

—*Don Nathanson*

The Eternal Return

EDITORS' NOTE: Eric Knight was an army major in World War II. In January 1943, his transport plane was shot down en route to North Africa. Knight did not survive the crash.

A British-American, he left behind on his Pennsylvania farm his widow, Jere Knight, and his beloved dog, Toots, a great companion and watchdog whose loyalty and adventures inspired Knight to write this story.

Toots died two years after her master, in April 1945, and is buried at the farm.

This story was first published in the *Saturday Evening Post* in 1938, a week before Christmas, and deeply moved a nation emerging from the Great Depression, a nation that needed faith in miracles and belief in dreams. In the years that followed, as the simple virtues and verities fell out of fashion, so, too, did this story, although it remains one of the most powerful dog stories ever written. Its original title was *Lassie Come Home.*

Neither Knight nor Toots lived to see their story become an immortal symbol of the fidelity of man and dog and of the eternal return.

The dog had met the boy by the school gate for five years. Now she couldn't understand that times were changed, and she wasn't supposed to be there anymore. But the boy knew.

So when he opened the door of the cottage, he spoke before he entered.

"Mother," he said, "Lassie's come home again."

He waited a moment, as if in hope of something. But the man and woman inside the cottage did not speak.

"Come in, Lassie," the boy said. He held open the

door, and the tricolor collie walked in obediently. Going head down, as a collie will when it knows something is wrong, it went to the rug and lay down before the hearth, a black-white-and-gold aristocrat. The man, sitting on a low stool by the fireside, kept his eyes turned away. The woman went to the sink and busied herself there.

"She were waiting at school for me, just like always," the boy went on. He spoke fast, as if racing against time. "She must ha' got away again. I thought, happen this time, we might just—"

"No!" the woman exploded.

The boy's carelessness dropped. His voice rose in pleading.

"But this time, Mother! Just this time. We could hide her. They wouldn't never know."

"Dogs, dogs, dogs!" the woman cried. The words poured from her as if the boy's pleading had been a signal gun for her own anger. "I'm sick o' hearing about tykes round this house. Well, she's sold and gone and done with, so the quicker she's taken back the better. Now get her back quick, or first thing ye know we'll have Hynes round here again. Mr. Hynes!"

Her voice sharpened in imitation of the Cockney accent of the south: " 'Hi know you Yorkshiremen and yer come-'ome dogs. Training yer dogs to come 'ome so's yer can sell 'em hover and hover again.'

"Well, she's sold, so ye can take her out o' my house and home to them as bought her!"

The boy's bottom lip crept out stubbornly, and there was silence in the cottage. Then the dog lifted its head and nudged the man's hand, as a dog will when asking for patting. But the man drew away and stared, silently, into the fire.

The boy tried again, with the ceaseless guile of a child, his voice coaxing.

"Look, Feyther, she wants thee to bid her welcome. Aye, she's that glad to be home. Happen they don't tak' good care on her up there? Look, her coat's a bit poorly, don't ye think? A bit o' linseed strained through her drinking water—that's what I'd gi' her."

Still looking in the fire, the man nodded. But the woman, as if perceiving the boy's new attack, sniffed.

"Aye, tha wouldn't be a Carraclough if tha didn't know more about tykes nor breaking eggs wi' a stick. Nor a Yorkshireman. My goodness, it seems to me sometimes that chaps in this village thinks more on their tykes nor they do o' their own flesh and blood. They'll sit by their firesides and let their own bairns starve so long as t' dog gets fed."

The man stirred, suddenly, but the boy cut in quickly.

"But she does look thin. Look, truly—they're not feeding her right. Just look!"

"Aye," the woman chattered. "I wouldn't put it past Hynes to steal t' best part o' t' dog meat for himself. And Lassie always was a strong eater."

"She's fair thin now," the boy said.

Almost unwillingly the man and woman looked at the dog for the first time.

"My gum, she is of a bit," the woman said. Then she caught herself. "Ma goodness, I suppose I'll have to fix her a bit o' summat. She can do wi' it. But soon as she's fed, back she goes. And never another dog I'll have in my house. Never another. Cooking and nursing for 'em, and as much trouble to bring up as a bairn!"

So, grumbling and chattering as a village woman will, she moved about, warming a pan of food for the dog. The man and boy watched the collie eat. When it was done, the boy took from the mantelpiece a folded cloth and a brush, and began prettying the collie's coat. The man watched for several minutes, and then could stand it no longer.

"Here," he said.

He took the cloth and brush from the boy and began working expertly on the dog, rubbing the rich, deep coat, then brushing the snowy whiteness of the full ruff and the apron, bringing out the heavy leggings on the forelegs. He lost himself in his work, and the boy sat on the rug, watching contentedly. The woman stood it as long as she could.

"Now will ye please tak' that tyke out o' here?"

The man flared in anger.

"Well, ye wouldn't have me tak' her back looking like a mucky Monday wash, wouldta?"

He bent again, and began fluffing out the collie's petticoats.

"Joe!" the woman pleaded. "Will ye tak' her out o' here? Hynes'll be nosing round afore ye know it. And I won't have that man in my house. Wearing his hat inside, and going on like he's the duke himself—him and his leggings!"

"All right, lass."

"And this time, Joe, tak' young Joe wi' ye."

"What for?"

"Well, let's get the business done and over with. It's him that Lassie runs away for. She comes for young Joe. So if he went wi' thee, and told her to stay, happen she'd be content and not run away no more, and then we'd have a little peace and quiet in the home—though heaven knows there's not much hope o' that these days, things being like they are." The woman's voice trailed away, as if she would soon cry in weariness.

The man rose. "Come, Joe," he said. "Get thy cap."

• • •

The duke of Rudling walked along the gravel paths of
his place with his granddaughter Philippa. Philippa was
a bright and knowing young woman, allegedly the only
member of the duke's family he could address in un-
spotted language. For it was also alleged that the duke
was the most irascible, vile-tempered old man in the
three Ridings of Yorkshire.

"Country going to pot!" the duke roared, stabbing at
the walk with his great blackthorn stick. "When I was a
young man! Hah! Women today not as pretty. Horses
today not as fast. As for dogs—ye don't see dogs today
like—"

Just then the duke and Philippa came round a clump
of rhododendrons and saw a man, a boy, and a dog.

"Ah," said the duke, in admiration. And then his
brow knotted. "Damme, Carraclough! What're ye doing with my dog?"

He shouted it quite as if the others were in the next
county, for it was also the opinion of the duke of
Rudling that people were not nearly so keen of hearing
as they used to be when he was a young man.

"It's Lassie," Carraclough said. "She runned away
again, and I brought her back."

Carraclough lifted his cap and poked the boy to do
the same, not in any servile gesture, but to show that
they were as well brought up as the next.

"Damme, ran away again!" the duke roared. "And I
told that utter nincompoop Hynes to—where is he?
Hynes! Hynes! Damme, Hynes, what're ye hiding for?"

"Coming, your lordship!" sounded a voice, far away
behind the shrubberies. And soon Hynes appeared, a
sharp-faced man in check coat, riding breeches, and the
cloth leggings that grooms wear.

"Take this dog," roared the duke, "and pen her up! And, damme, if she breaks out again, I'll—I'll—"

The duke waved his great stick threateningly, and then, without so much as a thank-you or kiss the back of the hand to Joe Carraclough, he went stamping and muttering away.

"I'll pen 'er up," Hynes muttered when the duke was gone. "And if she ever gets awye agyne, I'll—"

He made as if to grab the dog, but Joe Carraclough's hobnailed boot trod heavily on Hynes' foot.

"I brought my lad wi' me to bid her stay, so we'll pen her up this time. Eigh—sorry! I didn't see I were on thy foot. Come, Joe, lad."

They walked down the crunching gravel path, along by the neat kennel buildings. When Lassie was behind the closed door, she raced into the high wire run where she could see them as they went. She pressed close against the wire, waiting.

The boy stood close, too, his fingers through the meshes touching the dog's nose.

"Go on, lad," his father ordered. "Bid her stay!"

The boy looked around, as if for help that he did not find. He swallowed, and then spoke, low and quickly.

"Stay here, Lassie, and don't come home no more," he said. "And don't come to school for me no more. Because I don't want to see ye no more. 'Cause tha's a bad dog, and we don't love thee no more, and we don't want thee. So stay there forever and leave us be, and don't never come home no more."

Then he turned, and because it was hard to see the path plainly, he stumbled. But his father, who was holding his head very high as they walked away from Hynes, shook him savagely, and snapped roughly: "Look where tha's going!"

Then the boy trotted beside his father. He was thinking that he'd never be able to understand why grown-ups sometimes were so bad-tempered with you just when you needed them most.

After that, there were days and days that passed, and the dog did not come to the school gate anymore. So then it was not like old times. There were so many things that were not like old times.

The boy was thinking that as he came wearily up the path and opened the cottage door and heard his father's voice, tense with anger: "Walk my feet off. If tha thinks I like—"

Then they heard his opening of the door and the voice stopped and the cottage was silent.

That's how it was now, the boy thought. They stopped talking in front of you. And this, somehow, was too much for him to bear.

He closed the door, ran out into the night and onto the moor, that great flat expanse of land where all the people of that village walked in lonesomeness when life and its troubles seemed past bearing.

A long while later, his father's voice cut through the darkness.

"What's tha doing out here, Joe lad?"

"Walking."

"Aye."

They went on together, aimlessly, each following his own thoughts. And they both thought about the dog that had been sold.

"Tha maun't think we're hard on thee, Joe," the man said at last. "It's just that a chap's got to be honest. There's that to it. Sometimes, when a chap doesn't have much, he clings right hard to what he's got. And honest is honest, and there's no two ways about it.

"Why, look, Joe. Seventeen year I worked in that

Clarabelle Pit till she shut down, and a good collier too. Seventeen year! And butties I've had by the dozen, and never a man of 'em can ever say that Joe Carraclough kept what wasn't his, nor spoke what wasn't true. Not a man in this Riding can call a Carraclough mishonest.

"And when ye've sold a man summat, and ye've taken his brass, and ye've spent it—well, then done's done. That's all. And ye've got to stand by that."

"But Lassie was—"

"Now, Joe! Ye can't alter it, ever. It's done—and happen it's for t' best. No two ways, Joe, she were getting hard to feed. Why, ye wouldn't want Lassie to be going around getting peaked and pined, like some chaps round here keep their tykes. And ye're fond of her, then just think on that now she's got lots to eat, and a private kennel, and a good run to herself, and living like a varritable princess, she is. Ain't that best for her?"

"We wouldn't pine her. We've always got lots to eat."

The man blew out his breath angrily. "Eigh, Joe, nowt pleases thee. Well then, tha might as well have it. Tha'll never see Lassie no more. She run home once too often, so the duke's taken her wi' him up to his place in Scotland, and there she'll stay. So it's good-bye and good luck to her, and she'll never come home no more, she won't. Now, I weren't off to tell thee, but there it is, so put it in thy pipe and smoke it, and let's never say a word about it no more—especially in front of thy mother."

The boy stumbled on in the darkness. Then the man halted.

"We ought to be getting back, lad. We left thy mother alone."

He turned the boy about and then went on, but as if he were talking to himself.

"Tha sees, Joe, women's not like men. They have to

stay home and manage best they can, and just spend the time in wishing. And when things don't go right, well, they have to take it out in talk and give a man hell. But it don't mean nowt, really, so tha shouldn't mind when thy mother talks hard.

"Ye just got to learn to be patient and let 'em talk, and just let it go up t' chimney wi' th' smoke."

Then they were quiet, until, over the rise, they saw the lights of the village. Then the boy spoke: "How far away is Scotland, Feyther?"

"Nay, lad, it's a long, long road."

"But how far, Feyther?"

"I don't know—but it's a longer road than thee or me'll ever walk. Now, lad. Don't fret no more, and try to be a man—and don't plague thy mother no more, wilta?"

Joe Carraclough was right. It is a long road, as they say in the North, from Yorkshire to Scotland. Much too far for a man to walk—or a boy. And though the boy often thought of it, he remembered his father's words on the moor, and he put the thought behind him.

But there is another way of looking at it; and that's the distance from Scotland to Yorkshire. And that is just as far as from Yorkshire to Scotland. A matter of about four hundred miles, it would be, from the duke of Rudling's place far up in the Highlands down to the village of Holdersby. That would be for a man, who could go fairly straight.

To an animal, how much farther would it be? For a dog can study no maps, read no signposts, ask no directions. It could only go blindly, by instinct, knowing that it must keep on to the south, to the south. It would wander and err, quest and quarter, run into firths and lochs that would send it side-tracking and back-tracking before it could go again on its way—south.

A thousand miles, it would be, going that way—a thousand miles over strange terrain.

There would be moors to cross, and burns to swim. And then those great, long lochs that stretch almost from one side of that dour land to another would bar the way and send a dog questing a hundred miles before it could find a crossing that would allow it to go south.

And, too, there would be rivers to cross, wide rivers like the Forth and the Clyde, the Tweed and the Tyne, where one must go miles to find bridges. And the bridges would be in towns. And in the towns there would be officials—like the one in Lanarkshire. In all his life he had never let a captured dog get away— except one. That one was a gaunt, snarling collie that whirled on him right in the pound itself, and fought and twisted loose to race away down the city street— going south.

But there are also kind people, too; ones knowing and understanding in the ways of dogs. There was an old couple in Durham who found a dog lying exhausted in a ditch one night—lying there with its head to the south. They took that dog into their cottage and warmed it and fed it and nursed it. And because it seemed an understanding, wise dog, they kept it in their home, hoping it would learn to be content. But, as it grew stronger, every afternoon toward four o'clock it would go to the door and whine, and then begin pacing back and forth between the door and the window, back and forth as the animals do in their cages at the zoo.

They tried every wile and every kindness to make it bide with them, but finally, when the dog began to re- fuse food, the old people knew what they must do. Be- cause they understood dogs, they opened the door one afternoon, and they watched a collie go, not down the road to the right, or to the left, but straight across a field toward the south; going steadily at a trot, as if it knew it still had a long, long road to travel.

Ah, a thousand miles of tor and brae, of shire and moor, of path and road and plowland, of river and stream and burn and brook and beck, of snow and rain and fog and sun, is a long way, even for a human being. But it would seem too far—much, much too far—for any dog to travel blindly and win through.

And yet—and yet—who shall say why, when so many weeks had passed that hope against hope was dying, a boy coming out of school, out of the cloakroom that always smelled of damp wool drying, across the concrete play yard with the black, waxed slides, should turn his eyes to a spot by the school gate from force of five years of habit, and see there a dog? Not a dog, this one, that lifted glad ears above a proud, slim head with its black-and-gold mask; but a dog that lay weakly, trying to lift a head that would no longer lift, trying to wag a tail that was torn and blotched and matted with dirt and burs, and managing to do nothing much except to whine in a weak, happy, crying way as a boy on his knees threw arms about it, and hands touched it that had not touched it for many a day.

Then who shall picture the urgency of a boy, running, awkwardly, with a great dog in his arms—running through the village, past the empty mill, past the Labor Exchange, where the men looked up from their deep ponderings on life and the dole? Or who shall describe the high tones of a voice—a boy's voice, calling as he runs up a path: "Mother! Oh, Mother! Lassie's come home! Lassie's come home!"

Nor does anyone who ever owned a dog need to be told the sounds a man makes as he bends over a dog that has been his for many years; or how a woman moves quickly, preparing food, which might be the family's condensed milk stirred into warm water; or how the jowl of a dog is lifted so that raw egg and brandy, bought with precious pence, should be spooned in; or how bleeding pads are bandaged, tenderly.

That was one day. There was another day when the woman in the cottage sighed with pleasure, for a dog lifted itself to its feet for the first time to stand over a bowl of oatmeal, putting its head down and lapping again and again while its pinched flanks quivered.

And there was another day when the boy realized that, even now, the dog was not to be his again. So the cottage rang again with protests and cries, and a woman shrilling: "Is there never to be no more peace in my house and home?" Long after he was in bed that night the boy heard the rise and fall of the woman's voice, and the steady, reiterative tone of the man's. It went on long after he was asleep.

In the morning the man spoke, not looking at the boy, saying the words as if he had long rehearsed them.

"Thy mother and me have decided upon it that Lassie shall stay here till she's better. Anyhow, nobody could nurse her better than us. But the day that t' duke comes back, then back she goes, too. For she belongs to him and that's honest, too. Now tha has her for a while, so be content."

In childhood, "for a while" is such a great stretch of days when seen from one end. It is a terribly short time seen from the other.

The boy knew how short it was that morning as he went to school and saw a motorcar driven by a young woman. And in the car was a gray-thatched, terrible old man, who waved a cane and shouted: "Hi! Hi, there! Damme, lad! You there! Hi!"

Then it was no use running, for the car could go

faster than you, and soon it was beside you and the man was saying: "Damme, Philippa, will you make this smelly thing stand still a moment? Hi, lad!"

"Yes, sir."

"You're What's-'is-Name's lad, aren't you?"

"Ma feyther's Joe Carraclough."

"I know. I know. Is he home now?"

"No, sir. He's away to Allerby. A mate spoke for him at the pit and he's gone to see if there's a chance."

"When'll he be back?"

"I don't know. I think about tea."

"Eh, yes. Well, yes. I'll drop round about fivish to see that father of yours. Something important."

It was hard to pretend to listen to lessons. There was only waiting for noon. Then the boy ran home.

"Mother! T' duke is back and he's coming to take Lassie away."

"Eigh, drat my buttons. Never no peace in this house. Is tha sure?"

"Aye. He stopped me. He said tell Feyther he'll be round at five. Can we hide her? Oh, Mother."

"Nay, thy feyther—"

"Won't you beg him? Please, please. Beg Feyther to—"

"Young Joe, now it's no use. So stop thy teasing! Thy feyther'll not lie. That much I'll give him. Come good, come bad, he'll not lie."

"But just this once, Mother. Please beg him, just this once. Just one lie wouldn't hurt him. I'll make it up to him. I will. When I'm growed up, I'll get a job. I'll make money. I'll buy him things—and you, too. I'll buy you both anything you want if you'll only—"

For the first time in his trouble the boy became a child, and the mother, looking over, saw the tears that ran openly down his contorted face. She turned her face to the fire, and there was a pause. Then she spoke.

"Joe, tha mustn't," she said softly. "Tha must learn never to want nothing in life like that. It don't do, lad. Tha mustn't want things bad, like tha wants Lassie."

The boy shook his clenched fists in impatience.

"It ain't that, Mother. Ye don't understand. Don't ye see—it ain't me that wants her. It's her that wants us! That's what made her come all them miles. It's her that wants us, so terrible bad!"

The woman turned and stared. It was as if, in that moment, she were seeing this child, this boy, this son of her own, for the first time in many years. She turned her head down toward the table. It was surrender.

"Come and eat, then," she said. "I'll talk to him. I will that, all right. I feel sure he won't lie. But I'll talk to him, all right. I'll talk to Mr. Joe Carraclough. I will indeed!"

At five that afternoon, the duke of Rudling, fuming and muttering, got out of a car at a cottage gate to find a boy barring his way. This was a boy who stood, stubbornly, saying fiercely: "Away wi' thee! Thy tyke's net here!"

"Damme, Philippa, th' lad's touched," the duke said. "He is. He's touched."

Scowling and thumping his stick, the old duke advanced until the boy gave way, backing down the path out of the reach of the waving blackthorn stick.

"Thy tyke's net here," the boy protested.

"What's he saying?" the girl asked.

"Says my dog isn't here. Damme, you going deaf? I'm supposed to be deaf, and I hear him plainly enough. Now, ma lad, what tyke o' mine's net here?"

As he turned to the boy, the duke spoke in broadest

Yorkshire, as he did always to the people of the cot-
tages—a habit which the duchess of Rudling, and many
more members of the duke's family, deplored.

"Coom, coom, ma lad. Whet tyke's net here?"

"No tyke o' thine. Us hasn't got it." The words began running faster and faster as the boy backed away
from the fearful old man who advanced. "No tyke
could have done it. No tyke can come all them miles. It
isn't Lassie. It's another one that looks like her. It isn't
Lassie!"

"Why, bless ma heart and sowl," the duke puffed.
"Where's thy father, ma lad?"

The door behind the boy opened, and a woman's
voice spoke.

"If it's Joe Carraclough ye want, he's out in the shed
and been there shut up half the afternoon."

"What's this lad talking about—a dog of mine being
here?"

"Nay," the woman snapped quickly. "He didn't say a
tyke o' thine was here. He said it wasn't here."

"Well, what dog o' mine isn't here, then?"

The woman swallowed, and looked about as if for
help. The duke stood, peering from under his jutting
eyebrows. Her answer, truth or lie, was never spoken,
for then they heard the rattle of a door opening, and a
man making a pursing sound with his lips, as he will
when he wants a dog to follow, and then Joe Carraclough's voice said: "This is t' only tyke us has here.
Does it look like any dog that belongs to thee?"

With his mouth opening to cry one last protest, the
boy turned. And his mouth stayed open. For there he
saw his father, Joe Carraclough, the collie fancier,
standing with a dog at his heels—a dog that sat at his
left heel patiently, as any well-trained dog should do—
as Lassie used to do. But this dog was not Lassie. In

fact, it was ridiculous to think of it at the same moment as you thought of Lassie.

For where Lassie's skull was aristocratic and slim, this dog's head was clumsy and rough. Where Lassie's ears stood in twin-lapped symmetry, this dog had one ear draggling and the other standing up Alsatian fashion in a way to give any collie breeder the cold shivers. Where Lassie's coat was rich tawny gold, this dog's coat had ugly patches of black; and where Lassie's apron was a billowing stretch of snow-white, this dog had puddles of off-color blue-merle mixture.

Besides, Lassie had four white paws, and this one had one paw white, two dirty-brown, and one almost black.

That is the dog they all looked at as Joe Carraclough stood there, having told no lie, having only asked a question. They all stood, waiting the duke's verdict.

But the duke said nothing. He only walked forward, slowly, as if he were seeing a dream. He bent beside the collie, looking with eyes that were as knowing about dogs as any Yorkshireman alive. And those eyes did not waste themselves upon twisted ears, or blotched marking, or rough head. Instead they were looking at a paw that the duke lifted, looking at the underside of the paw, staring intently at five black pads, crossed and recrossed with the scars where thorns had lacerated, and stones had torn.

For a long time the duke stared, and when he got up he did not speak in Yorkshire accents anymore. He spoke as a gentleman should, and he said: "Joe Carraclough. I never owned this dog. 'Pon my soul, she's never belonged to me. Never!"

Then he turned and went stumping down the path, thumping his cane and saying: "Bless my soul. Four hundred miles! Damme, wouldn't ha' believed it. Damme—five hundred miles!"

He was at the gate when his granddaughter whispered to him fiercely.

"Of course," he cried. "Mind your own business. Exactly what I came for. Talking about dogs made me forget. Carraclough! Carraclough! What're ye hiding for?"

"I'm still here, sir."

"Ah, there you are. You working?"

"Eigh, now. Working," Joe said. That's the best he could manage.

"Yes, working, working!" the duke fumed.

"Well, now—" Joe began.

Then Mrs. Carraclough came to his rescue, as a good housewife in Yorkshire will.

"Why, Joe's got three or four things that he's been considering," she said, with proper display of pride. "But he hasn't quite said yes or no to any of them yet."

"Then say no, quick," the old man puffed. "Had to sack Hynes. Didn't know a dog from a drunken filly.

"Should ha' known all along no Londoner could handle dogs fit for Yorkshire taste. How much, Carraclough?"

"Well, now," Joe began.

"Seven pounds a week, and worth every penny," Mrs. Carraclough chipped in. "One o' them other offers may come up to eight," she lied, expertly. For there's always a certain amount of lying to be done in life, and when a woman's married to a man who has made a lifelong cult of being honest, then she's got to learn to do the lying for two.

"Five," roared the duke—who, after all, was a Yorkshireman, and couldn't help being a bit sharp about things that pertained to money.

"Six," said Mrs. Carraclough.

"Five pound ten," bargained the duke, cannily.

"Done," said Mrs. Carraclough, who would have settled for three pounds in the first place. "But, o' course, us gets the cottage too."

"All right," puffed the duke. "Five pounds ten and the cottage. Begin Monday. But on one condition. Carraclough, you can live on my land, but I won't have that thick-skulled, screw-lugged, gay-tailed eyesore of a misshapen mongrel on my property. Now never let me see her again. You'll get rid of her?"

He waited, and Joe fumbled for words. But it was the boy who answered, happily, gaily: "Oh, no, sir. She'll be waiting at school for me most o' the time. And, anyway, in a day or so we'll have her fixed up so's ye'd never, never recognize her."

"I don't doubt that," puffed the duke, as he went to the car. "I don't doubt ye could do just exactly that."

A long time afterward, the girl said: "Don't sit there like a lion on the Nelson column. I thought you were supposed to be a hard man."

"Fiddlesticks, m'dear. I'm a ruthless realist. For five years I've sworn I'd have that dog by hook or crook, and now, egad, at last I've got her."

"Pooh! You had to buy the man before you could get his dog."

"Well, perhaps that's not the worst part of the bargain."

—*Eric Knight*

CHAPTER FOUR

Hope and Perseverance

Near this spot are deposited the remains of one who possessed beauty without vanity, strength without insolence, courage without ferocity, and all the virtues of Man, without his vices. This praise, which would be unmeaning flattery if inscribed over human ashes, is but a just tribute to the memory of Boatswain, a dog.

—Lord Byron, inscription on the monument of his Newfoundland dog, Boatswain (1808)

Brandy

This is a story about two extraordinary people and a very special dog. I read about this story in my local paper and was so impressed that I contacted the couple to tell them how I felt. That's how I came to know Tony and Diana Crimi and their dog Brandy. The article I read only began to touch this remarkable story of sacrifice and love of animals.

It all began around May of 1995 in Roy, Washington. Like many towns in Washington, Roy is a mix of wild woods and urban sprawl. Wildlife abounds. One day Diana was driving past a particularly wild area when she noticed a very young hunting dog. She attempted to catch her but the dog was terrified. When she got home she told Tony about it and through their concern, they began leaving dog food out every day along this five-mile stretch of highway. From May through September, every day, Diana and Tony left food for a wild dog they hardly ever saw. In fact, Diana saw the dog only three or four times. All efforts to coax her to them failed.

By September, Diana was getting really worried. Although she was now able to approach the dog to within fifteen feet, it was apparent she was starving to death. Her ribs stood out in stark relief and her spine was distinct from head to tail. By October, although Diana had been feeding Brandy daily, the dog would wait in the brush and eat only after she left. Diana and Tony tried to use food to lure Brandy into a humane cage trap, but Brandy never came near it.

Diana also could see that the dog had a training collar on her. It had apparently been placed on her at a very young age, because the collar was too small, cutting into the skin, and she had a serious infection. The swelling under her chin was the size of a grapefruit; and even at fifteen feet, Diana could smell the decay.

Daily she carried food in hopes of catching a glimpse of Brandy (so christened by the Crimis).

Winter was coming, and in that area it can be cruelly harsh. In October, Diana and Tony went searching on foot through the woods. They found a den of sorts, an area under an old viaduct near railroad tracks. Now they began bringing the food directly to the den. Diana also left an article of clothing each time in hopes that Brandy would get used to her smell.

But Brandy disappeared for long periods—ten days in October, fourteen days in December, thirteen days in February.

Other people became aware of her plight. When a cage was placed at her den, she disappeared and didn't return.

Starvation and infection were a daily menace for Brandy—and the Crimis were close to panic. Then Brandy was spotted along highway 507. The news brought both cheer and dread to Diana because that area is particularly dangerous to wildlife. Food was again left out.

Being able to hold off the starvation brought about a new concern. Diana was fearful that the collar, now deeply imbedded in her neck, would eventually strangle her. They continued to care for her from a distance. Infection after infection raged around her neck, and a pouch developed from the skin that could not subside back to normal. Diana contacted a local vet at the military base who gave her antibiotics. This was put in the dog's food.

By the spring of 1996, the Crimis were getting desperate. Brandy had managed to survive several encounters with coyotes, a mother bear and her two cubs, major flooding, heavy traffic, and a freezing winter of rain and snow. But it was only a matter of time before her luck ran out. So Tony built a special cage.

They found an area she frequented in the woods and set up. They placed food closer and closer to the cage. Five long days passed. Finally, Tony rigged a camouflage net and climbed up into a tree. After four hours of patiently waiting, Brandy walked into the net area to eat and Tony pulled.

Brandy, terrified, fought to get away. Then the Crimis touched her and said what a good girl she was. She looked at Tony, gave three tail wags, and gave up her battle with fear.

Nearly a year had passed since Diana first saw Brandy. They discovered that the collar had rotted off but the continued infection had done serious damage. The vet performed several surgeries to repair the hole in her neck and gave her copious quantities of antibiotics to clear up the infections. He estimated her age, and Tony and Diana were horrified to realize that Brandy began this ordeal at the tender age of seven months.

Cleaned up, Brandy was intensely curious, active, gentle, and very affectionate—a rangy dog with black lop ears and a white, short-haired coat with black spots. She was healthy except for the earlier neck infection and a pink scar where the collar used to be.

Diana and Tony believe she's an English pointer. A breeder of such dogs moved away from the area in the winter. The electronic shock collar she had on was like those worn by hunting dogs in field trials. Diana and others believed Brandy fled from a field-trial area nearby.

Today, she is healthy and happy. She rarely leaves Tony's side.

I am continually amazed when I reflect on this remarkable dog who had such tremendous heart and courage.

As someone who frequently rescues stray dogs, I would like to think I would have gone to the lengths that the Crimis did. But I'm not sure. They are wonderful people with hearts bigger than normal.

If only everyone had their compassion and capacity to give, how much better our world would be.

"It's a miracle she wasn't killed," Diana said. "It's such a happy ending. All she needed was someone to touch her and love her."

After struggling to escape that first night, Brandy had simply lain down, tired. Afterward, she jumped into Diana and Tony's truck and slept in Diana's lap all the way home.

—Deborah M. Killian

Puppies for Sale

A store owner was tacking a sign in his store window which read PUPPIES FOR SALE, when a little boy appeared.

"How much are you selling the puppies for?" he asked.

The man told the lad he didn't expect to let any of them go for less than $50.

The boy reached in his pocket, pulled out some change, looked up at the store owner and said, "I have two dollars and thirty-seven cents. Can I look at them?"

The store owner smiled and whistled. From the kennel, a dog named Lady came running down the aisle, followed by five tiny balls of fur. One puppy lagged behind. Immediately, the little boy asked about the limping puppy.

"What's wrong with that doggie?"

"The veterinarian told us the dog is missing a hip socket," said the store owner. "He'll always limp like that."

"That's the one I want to buy," the lad said quickly.

The store owner replied, "No, you don't want to buy that dog. If you really want him, I'll just give him to you."

The boy came close to the store owner's face and said angrily, "I don't want you to just *give* him to me. That doggie is worth just as much as all the other puppies and I'll pay the full price. In fact, I'll give you $2.37 now and 50¢ a month until I have him paid for!"

The store owner replied, "No, no, no. You don't want that dog. He's never going to be able to run and jump and play like the other dogs."

In response, the little boy pulled up his pant leg to reveal a badly twisted left leg, supported by two steel braces.

"Well, sir," he said, "I don't run so well myself and the puppy will need someone who understands."

—*Dan Clark*

Pennies for Balto

Everyone knows how Balto saved the children of Nome, Alaska, from a diphtheria epidemic. Less well known is how the children of Cleveland saved Balto.

In 1927, George Kimball, a Cleveland businessman, was visiting Los Angeles when he saw eight Siberian husky dogs in a cheap side-show window. The exhibit upset him. The dogs were chained up. With their heavy, arctic coats, they suffered in the California heat and were cared for poorly.

George was astonished to learn that one of the dogs was Balto, and the others were part of the sled team that Balto had led only two years earlier to save the people of Nome from a diphtheria epidemic. George couldn't afford the two thousand dollars needed to buy the sled-dog team, so he appealed to the people of Cleveland.

Today, in Central Park in New York City there stands a bronze statue of Balto, Gunnar Kaasen's lead dog. On its base is the inscription:

Dedicated to the indomitable
Spirit of sled dogs that relayed
Antitoxin six hundred miles
Over rough ice, across treacherous
Waters, through Arctic
Blizzards, from Nenana to the
Relief of stricken Nome in the
Winter of 1925. Endurance . . .
Fidelity . . . Intelligence . . .

Today, Balto's heroics are well known. On January 20, 1925, the only doctor in Nome telegraphed

Anchorage that a diphtheria outbreak was threatening thousands of lives, and he was out of serum. Two pilots volunteered to fly it in but that was deemed too dangerous. The only way to get antitoxin to the city was by dog sled from Nenana, 674 miles away.

As the world watched, the trek took five days, seven and one-half hours. Twenty mushers and 150 dogs formed a relay. Five children died, twenty-nine cases of diphtheria were diagnosed, and eleven hundred people were threatened with the epidemic. Balto led the team across the last fifty-three miles, taking his musher, temporarily blinded and unable to stand, to the door of Nome's only physician.

When spring 1925 came to Nome, there were children there, historians have written, largely because of "endurance, fidelity, intelligence."

When Balto was in need, the children of Cleveland were his heroes.

Upon returning to Cleveland, George organized a major fund-raising campaign—pennies for Balto.

"As you came into school with your pennies, you put them in the bowl before you went to your classroom," Garnet Bielfelt told National Public Radio many years later. "There was just one big bowl. And you know, children in those days did not think of stealing or anything else. They were so proud to put their pennies in the bowl. We just were happy to see that bowl get bigger and bigger."

More than twenty-three hundred dollars was raised and Balto and his team were given a hero's parade in Cleveland and a home at the Cleveland zoo. Fifteen thousand people turned out the first day to see the dogs.

"Something about Balto kind of drew me and I stepped over that rope and went up to Balto and touched him just briefly," Garnet remembered. "At least I got to touch Balto. That was a big thrill."

In fact, the people of Cleveland loved Balto so much that when he died in 1933, he was stuffed. Today he stands in the natural history museum as though peering through a blizzard searching for Nome.

"His eyes still sparkle," Garnet said, "he still has that look in his eye that he had when he was alive. They didn't take that away from him."

—Michael Capuzzo

The Christmas Miracle

In rural Indiantown, Florida, innkeeper Jonnie Wall Williams collects Christmas miracles.

"I learned early to seek miracles and record them," said Williams, who likes to say she's descended from "a long line of cooks and storytellers."

"Miracles come in all sizes," said Jonnie, an Indiantown native who owns and runs the Seminole Inn. "Sometimes miracles are lessons life teaches," she said. "Sometimes they come in very big ways—and sometimes in very small, subtle ways—like the thought that tells you to do something."

Jonnie, forty-three, shares her miracle stories each year with guests at the historic inn's Christmas parties.

From growing up on an Indiantown ranch in a "very happy home, riding all day long until dark," she recalled a Christmas miracle from childhood.

"I had a horse named Flicka and a dog named Wrinkles, a boxer puppy. We called him Wrinkles because his face got all wrinkled up when he smiled at you, the way dogs will do."

When Flicka was sold to a family in town, Wrinkles moved to town with the horse. Jonnie missed Wrinkles—until that first Christmas, when he came home. "He came home every Christmas after that, too. We used to wonder how he knew what day it was, but he did."

Years later, Jonnie, newly divorced, had moved back home with her parents. Son Josh, then ten, had taken the divorce "very, very hard." He wanted a dog for Christmas. "I told him no, we couldn't get a dog, not while we were living with his grandparents. He begged. I said no."

Christmas morning, Josh galloped outside and came back, eyes big as saucers, to ask, "Who got me the dog?"

Nobody did. "Girl was the community dog. She just decided she was our dog and came to our house because Josh needed her. She's a little red cur dog and she just adored Josh."

Girl stayed with the family six months or so, and then moved on, "took up with someone else who needed her," Jonnie said.

"Josh and the dog made me realize how significant

prayers and wishes of people are. You try to apply adult logic to these things, and it just doesn't work."

—*Sally D. Swartz*

The Feisty Teacher

Winter winds were still whipping western Montana well into the second week of April 1975. Throughout the long winter, I had entertained a dream of buying a registered malamute or Akita puppy in the spring. I visualized this finely bred puppy growing into a dog that would pull me up the rugged trails of the Selway-Bitterroot Wilderness while carrying his own food in a backpack.

I had lost both legs to a mortar shell while serving with the Marine Corps in Korea. This dream dog was to be my way of gaining access to the back country.

When I told my wife of my plans, she nodded and continued to work on a painting which she was completing, but that night at dinner she said, "You know, somebody will always be waiting in line to buy those expensive animals in the pet shops, but most of the puppies in the animal shelter will die." She said no more, but I began to rethink my dream. I had been left with no hope of living once; perhaps this memory gave me a deeper insight.

The next morning I drove to the Missoula Humane Society. "I need a special puppy," I told the young woman at the counter, "one that will be able to carry a heavy pack in the hills."

The woman's smile faded. "I'll show you the only puppy we have left. Someone came in yesterday and left this little fellow. I fell in love with him; I tried to feed him, with no success, but there is something special about him."

Before I could tell her to forget it, she was through the door, and there I was in the cold waiting room wishing I had gone to the pet shop on the south side of town.

The woman returned with the saddest emaciated puppy I had ever seen. His tail was almost bare and hung like a winter twig. His head drooped and a tiny rib cage protruded through thin skin. His hide was pink where the hair was gone. I reached out and raised his head. He looked at me, but all hope was gone from his blue eyes. This was no vigorous sled dog to be sure, but I felt an instant rush of rapport with this deserted puppy. "I'll take him," I said.

"You'll take him?" the woman asked, beaming.

"Of course I'll take him," I answered, more composed now.

The woman brought out a paper, which I signed. "That will be ten dollars," she said, still smiling. She turned to the puppy, who could barely stand, and lifted his head and tail. "Hold up your tail," she whispered. "You've been adopted."

His tail remained slightly curled over his back as I carried him in my jacket to the station wagon. On the way home I massaged his ears gently and told him I expected great things of him, but he did not respond. When I got home, my wife met me at the door. "My goodness," she murmured, "he's pink."

"Oh, he's a little pink, all right," I admitted, "but look at those eyes. There's steel in those blue eyes." Little did I know.

After a few days of intensive care, those blue eyes did show a spark, and we named him Feist. For several days we thought Feist was retarded because he did not respond to any sounds; then one morning my wife had a hunch. "I believe Feist could be deaf," she said. She took him into the garage and blew a shrill whistle. Feist just sat on his blanket and looked at my wife with a vacant stare. He was totally deaf.

During the following six weeks Feist filled out and gained new strength. His tail became a bushy plume, which he wagged proudly. He seemed to like being outside even in the cold early spring, so I built him an insulated doghouse, lining it with blankets, which he promptly shredded. He ripped perennials from their beds, dug newly planted potatoes from their hills, and ravaged the strawberry bed. He even wrenched the lower limbs from small trees. My previous compassion began to wane. I became defensive. I fenced the garden, tied up what was left of the fruit trees, and nailed down a new mat in his house. I even thought of placing an ad in the local paper: "Beautiful Australian shepherd puppy—reasonable."

The last week of May arrived, and I was busy preparing and grading final exams, when the special education director for our school district called. "I'd like for you to come and visit some of my special education students," she said. "I think you might be an inspiration to them."

"What do you mean?" I asked. "How am I supposed to inspire special ed students?"

"You seem to have overcome your disability," she answered, "and you seem to walk rather well."

I was flattered. "Well, maybe I'll try to think of something. When is all this to take place and where do I go?"

"Could you be at Hawthorne School sometime Monday morning?"

"Monday morning, huh?" I mumbled.

"Oh, thank you so much," she said. There was a metallic click and silence.

All day Saturday and Sunday I wrote minispeeches on scratch paper, crumpled them, and threw them in the trash. What could I possibly say to these young people with whom I had so little in common? I thought of my own trials, but I had never faced a problem of this nature from birth. I grew more uneasy.

I was still pondering my problem when my wife announced dinner. I was just sixteen hours away from making a fool of myself. As I passed the end of the table, a gray-blue blur shot past the patio door in hot pursuit of a low-flying bird. "That's it," I shouted. "I've got a deaf puppy, and he's overcoming his handicap with a vengeance."

I begged two other teachers to cover my morning classes, put a leash on a squirming Feist, and headed for Hawthorne School.

The halls were quiet when we arrived, but I found the special ed room easily.

We were greeted with "ooohs and aaahs" as Feist and I entered the room. I turned to greet one of the teachers when a small boy in a wheelchair tugged at my sleeve. "I'm going to die in a few weeks, you know," he said. I swallowed hard and looked back at Feist.

A little girl who had been lying on the floor tried to rise, but fell back. A thin boy who lay on a covered table strained to get a better look at Feist. My mind went blank. I looked down at Feist, who stood in the middle of the room looking from one wheelchair to another. Why don't you just wag your tail, I thought.

Suddenly, as if he had read my thoughts, Feist tilted his head to one side, raised his tail, wagged it several times, and leaped through the air into the lap of the boy who had said he was going to die. He licked the boy's face and pulled at his hair. The boy laughed until tears fell on his faded shirt. Feist whirled and bounded to the girl on the floor who had now raised herself to a sitting position. He knocked her flat and began tugging at her blouse the same way he had ripped out my strawberry plants. He darted and whirled from one child to another until the room was filled with laughing children and cavorting puppy. Abruptly he stopped at the doorway and wagged his tail as if to say, "Show's over, guys."

I still could think of nothing to say. I mumbled a thanks to the teachers for inviting us, but I was thinking of an old vaudeville saying: "Never follow a dog act."

Amid cheers, I led Feist toward the main entrance. There was one pillar in the center of the hall, and just as the young principal entered the hallway, Feist lifted his leg and sprinkled the column liberally. The principal stiffened, and I felt my face get hot, but behind us I heard a chorus of "Yea, Feist!"

Feist grew, in understanding as well as in stature. He learned to play ball and became a true athlete. When he leaped high for a long one, his body would arch through the air like a rainbow trout rising to a fly in the Bitterroot River. He learned that trees were not to be torn apart, that the forced air from heat ducts was not an invisible foe, that birds could not be caught in flight. But more important, he studied my every move and learned to adjust to my limitations. He would tilt his head to one side and study my gait, but he tested and challenged me always.

When I finally decided it was time for our first walk, I bought a new leash and braced myself.

He waited impatiently until I had a firm grasp on the leash, then he leaned into the collar like a sled dog on his first race. I was launched into a half trot. I had not walked, if it could be called that, since Korea. I tried to slow him down, but he would have none of that. His trim legs churned and I lurched on in reluctant pursuit.

After nearly three weeks of this daily routine of at least a mile each day, I noticed that my breathing was easier and my legs were getting stronger. I began to look forward to our outings. Something akin to mild euphoria filled me for the first time in many years. I began to sniff the late spring air and enjoy the pungent smell of budding cottonwood. Sometimes Feist would pause to analyze some faint odor on the still morning air. There were times when we would take a break beside a stream; he would play at fishing for a floating leaf, looking back to see if I was watching his cavorting. The antics were not wasted. I learned to use new muscles by watching his graceful side-stepping. More important, I was now focusing more on him each day and less on myself. I began to realize that he was training me as a coach would prime an awkward child.

When we came to a deep stream, he would reconnoiter the bank and find a shallow place where I could cross, then splash to the other side, tail wagging furiously while I carefully chose the flattest rocks for footing. He showed me the easiest way around boulders and strained to pull me up steep inclines. He seemed to know my weaknesses, but he would tolerate no slacking on my part. If he was going to work at teaching, I would have to work at learning.

Feist accepted me as I was, but he challenged me to become my best self, to grow as he was growing, mentally and physically. Having no legs was no more an excuse for me than not hearing was an excuse for him.

For almost eighteen years, he showed indomitable courage. In his entire life he never once whined, whimpered, or complained in any way. He accepted life as it was, faced it squarely, and never backed away from anything or anyone.

Feist finally died in June of 1992, but he left behind a legacy: "Catch me if you can, and I'll teach you and be your shepherd." He is on the other side of the river now, tail wagging, eyes sparkling, beckoning to me to follow by treading on the deeply bedded rocks.

This is the true story of a remarkable dog who literally lifted my life several degrees. He was (and still is) an inspiration to me; because of his leadership, I still walk one and a half to two miles up and down hills each day. Feist is largely responsible for my present health and well-being.

I built a memorial to Feist in our backyard and my wife planted a flower garden around it. We give to the local animal shelter each month in his name so that other tails may wag and other people will learn.

We can't expect a perfect infant every time, but we can take what we are given and allow it to teach us to grow and blossom. This is what Feist taught.

—John M. Alston

The Seeing-Eye Person

Chelsa, our courageous Labrador, was a robust and enthusiastic working dog who for seven blissful years lived for the hours spent retrieving sticks and dummies from our lake. Then, tragedy struck the life of my gentle friend in the guise of diabetes. While we were working to adjust the amount of insulin, her eyesight began to fail. The clouds in both eyes darkened like foreboding black clouds overhead that threaten the onset of a severe storm. The storm struck, leaving Chelsa totally blind.

Our friends urged us to be humane and put Chelsa to sleep. Some scoffed at the expense we were willing to accept to keep her alive. She requires a special diet and insulin injections twice daily. I must admit that there were days when I wondered if I was being selfish by refusing to consider euthanasia.

Then Chelsa would hear my footsteps as I entered the room and begin to wag her tail with all the enthusiasm of a sighted dog. There she sat, still the watchman of the ball . . . ever ready to retrieve it should someone stop to play. I knew I could not take her life when she was so full of the joy of living.

Chelsa has a physical handicap. I am a physical therapist. My son has a physical handicap. All my patients have physical handicaps. If I believe so strongly in teaching my son and patients to overcome their handicaps, why should I doubt my ability to teach Chelsa to meet the challenge presented by her blindness?

I had experience working with blind children, so I understood the basic principles of teaching mobility. I decided to do my best to give Chelsa the opportunity to overcome the roadblock fate forced across her path.

My first stop was the toy store. I searched for balls and stuffed animals that made noise. I found a ball that rattled and jingle bells to put inside of whiffle balls. The stuffed animal with a hidden music box would be a perfect substitute for Chelsa's silent stuffed bear that she could no longer locate. Next, I found sugar-free doggy treats at the pet shop, which could be offered after painful insulin injections and tied to sticks as an aid in smelling for them.

The next step involved teaching Chelsa some new commands. *Up* and *down* would be given as a warning for stairs. *Watch out!* became an effective way to warn of an object in her path such as a tree or parked car. Directional cues included *here, back, no,* and *there it is*. I learned to snap my fingers or clap constantly while walking so Chelsa could follow me or find me. We warn *shot* before we inject her so as not to frighten her. And we avoid rearranging furniture or leaving the vacuum cleaner out.

Chelsa's world is safe again. She still guards her ball and waits in expectation for someone to throw it. She swims in water she cannot see and retrieves sticks with all the ardor of a sighted Lab. She follows me around the yard, successfully navigating around obstacles. She anticipates the steps and furniture because she remembers where these permanent obstacles are.

Chelsa is an inspiration to me as a physical therapist. If I can modify her environment and teach her new ways of approaching tasks successfully, then I can expect even more from my human patients. She is an inspiration to my son. Shane graduated from college this summer and entered graduate school. As he watches her struggle to continue participation in the activities she loves, he is encouraged in his personal struggle to be an active, contributing member of the adult world.

Chelsa brings out the best in all of us. She taught us to look for the value of life; she helped us look past the physical problems. She is a living example of perseverance against all odds. I have taken this experience to the nursing home where I teach older people that they do not have to quit living just because they face new physical challenges in the most vulnerable of their years. I have learned new tools to use in my quest to reach people others have given up on. Every time she returns triumphant, dripping wet with a stick held proudly in her mouth, I look deep into her vacant eyes and see her lion's heart.

—Patty Aguirre

Radar Finds a Loving Family

Hurricane Andrew destroyed their country home and forced them to relocate to a small apartment in a Miami suburb. Jim and Sherry Norris and their son, Scott, six, took a few boxes of belongings and their two mutts, Gipper and Cindy.

Jim spent many lunch hours watching their country home being rebuilt and feeding the stray Dobermans and shepherds who wandered up to the doorless garage. After a few days the strays were gone.

But shortly after moving back into their rebuilt home, Sherry opened the front door to see why her dogs were barking and saw a yellow shape dash across the street into the rejuvenating mango grove.

For several months the elusive stray was seen roaming the neighborhood fields. Scott spotted him one morning sunning in the middle of the road and said he looked more like a fox than a dog.

One October evening, Sherry was walking the fields, marveling at the restored grove—and there, in the moonlight, stood the stray yellow dog. "He froze as I walked slowly toward him," Sherry said. "I saw how pitifully thin he was. His huge ears were alert, tail curled over his back, hair straight up on his neck. I stopped and softly called to him. He turned and ran across the street. The next morning the yellow dog watched from his burrow as we went to school."

The next evening, Sherry left a pile of dog food at the corner. The yellow dog never appeared, but the next morning the food was gone. For days this routine continued.

"One evening I saw him approach the food," she said. "Each paw was slowly, carefully placed as if he were walking on eggs. He dropped his head and carefully chewed, watching me with wary eyes."

Halloween was approaching. "Now as I fed him he circled me and barked. It was a bluff, he was timid and frightened of people. My goal was to get close enough to get a collar and leash on him so he could be picked up by the animal control officer. His condition was pitiful, and I didn't want him near my child or dogs."

By Halloween, the dog was eating on the walkway to the house. In the mornings, Sherry now yelled "Dog!"

and a yellow dog, tail tucked between his legs, climbed out of his nest in the mango grove and slowly approached the house for breakfast.

"After months of feeding him, we named him Radar. Before long, Radar responded to his name. He looked less emaciated. His tail stayed tucked between his legs, but he was growing bolder.

"One November evening," Sherry said, "he reached out and put his paw on my hand. He watched as I stroked his offered limb. A few days later I could pet his head.

"Scott now joined me at the evening feeding, but the dog wouldn't let him get too near. One morning Radar decided Scott could be trusted. He lifted his paw and held it out to him.

"Jim was the next trusted human. Radar met him during lunchtime and offered his paw. It was about that time that Jim made his no more animals edict. Scott and I agreed Radar would remain outside. We couldn't help it when, as we unloaded groceries, he cautiously wandered into the house. When the phone rang the poor animal started shaking, and we realized he had never encountered one before. We shooed him out of the house before Jim came home.

"Radar now 'knocked' whenever he wanted to come in. The 'no more animals' edict was invoked again, and I promised to do something about Radar's future. We had to get him a home soon.

"I enlisted a neighbor to help me load him in the van for a trip to the veterinarian. Once he had a clean bill of health and was legally registered in Dade County, it was time for me to place a newspaper advertisement: 'Free to good home large, neutered male dog. Very sweet, needs a loving family.'

"After all the months of seeing him go from an emaciated, frightened animal to a not-quite-fat, learning-to-wag-his-tail, door-knocking dog, it would be hard to say good-bye.

"Scott couldn't understand why Radar couldn't stay with us. We pointed out we had two dogs, Radar wouldn't stay in our yard, and Daddy didn't like all the escape holes he dug. Radar had to go to a new family. Logical as it seemed to my husband and me, our child saw only the love he felt for the dog.

"The family came to our house to meet Radar in December. The mom, dad, and teenage daughter said he was a handsome dog, and my heart sank when they said they would take him. As they backed down the driveway his black nose was pressed against the window, and his eyes watched as Scott waved good-bye. The three of us walked back inside, adults silently telling themselves it was for the best, child heading sadly to his room. It was a very quiet Friday night.

"Saturday we received a phone call from his new family. He'd settled in nicely, was freshly bathed, and slept next to their daughter the previous night. He'd eaten and behaved in the house. They loved him.

"Sunday morning their next call came. He had escaped when the family had gone shopping for an hour. He'd used a bush to scale the five-foot wall that surrounded their home. I was horrified. Their home was approximately fifteen miles from us.

"City and county roads and the Florida Turnpike separated our areas. We knew what he was trying to do—come home. I was sick. My first impulse was to hop in the van and join the search. But I didn't want Scott to see the probable outcome, a dead dog. The guilt was immense. My poor little boy spent all day outside playing on the front lawn waiting for his friend to come home. I waited for the inevitable phone call to say that he had been found injured or dead.

"Five o'clock and still no word. I called them. They'd searched and driven around but could not find him. Dade County Animal Control was closed until Monday.

"That evening was the saddest in Scott's life. He reluctantly came in at sundown. When he said his prayers that night tears were in both our eyes. 'Please God, bring my Radar home. I love him so much, God, he's my friend,' prayed my little boy.

"Jim came home and he, too, was crushed by the news. As he climbed into bed he said if he makes it, we'll have to keep him. I got out of bed and walked through the darkened house through the kitchen and garage and out to the road. It was a dark mile of silence. The stars shone in a clear night sky, the promise of a Florida winter cooled the night breeze. Somewhere under the immense glittering sky was our poor lost Radar. I said my own prayer. It came from the little girl still alive in me who loves all the creatures who share our world. I've never asked for anything, I said to the sky, but please give us a Christmas miracle, please guide Radar home.

"Monday arrived with the weekday routine: dress, fix coffee, wake Scott for school. Jim wanted the sports page, I'd forgotten to get the newspaper. As the garage door slowly ground open I gasped—there in front of the door was our damp, lost dog. I yelled, 'He's back, he's back, Radar's back!' He trotted into the kitchen. Jim and Scott ran down the hall and hugs, licks, and a furiously wagging tail frenzy erupted. Then he drank a bowl of water, wolfed down a bowl of food, and collapsed on the floor. Our Christmas miracle really happened!

"Radar is a treasured family member now. We walk him three times a day. He has a great tracking nose, but the rabbits are safe. He has a very 'soft' mouth and even takes hand-fed treats delicately. In the morning he fills my vacated spot in bed, his head on my pillow. Since he has been a house dog his coat has turned to a beautiful shade of gold. He is forever our golden mutt."

—*Sherry Norris*

Give a Miracle to Get a Miracle

In the town of Cornelius, Oregon, there was a spirited old lady named Henrietta who was a walking ray of sunshine, making her rounds each morning on the town's sidewalks, gladdening all she met, while out in front of her galloped Daisy, the gap-toothed, pampas-grass-tailed, scruffy white dog.

Rain or shine the duo appeared, ever smiling, ever cheerful, ever enjoying their lives with each other and all they met.

Then one day Henrietta did not appear. And another. Still another. And the townspeople grew concerned, so some went to check and found Henrietta in a darkened room with a dying dog. Daisy was fog-eyed, her tongue protruding blue and limp between gapped teeth, her tousled coat without sheen.

These people who cared about Henrietta and Daisy insisted the dog be taken to the vet. The dog must be checked. For now it was revealed to the townspeople that Daisy was the generator of Henrietta's life.

Daisy was delivered to Dr. Bob Bullard, a middle-aged, casual-appearing but extremely precise and competent vet, who made an emergency examination. What he learned was serious. Daisy's ailment could be fatal, the treatment was costly, and Henrietta was without money—that's why she hadn't brought Daisy in.

Doc admitted Daisy to the hospital and started emergency medical care. Daisy would have to stay. So Henrietta trudged home with empty heart: spiritless, grave, without hope.

The next morning through the clinic door with a burst of self-purpose came a middle-aged woman who said to the doctor, "Pleased to meet you. I'm Henrietta's daughter . . . just come up from California when I heard about Daisy."

The woman slipped off her gloves and removed her coat. "Do you think the dog will live?" she asked the doctor.

And he turned to her with grave concern, for he heard more in her question than what she expressed. "Why do you ask?" he inquired.

"Because if Daisy would die, it really would be for the best. Mother is much too old to be up here in this wet Oregon weather gallivanting all around. With Daisy gone, we could convince Mom to come to California and live in a nursing home . . . give up this foolish independence. . . . It would be better really. So much better." She hesitated a moment, then asked, "Couldn't

Daisy just pass away?" Then, stammering, "It would relieve Daisy of all her pain and suffering."

Doc looked at the cold, steel examining table and thought of what would happen to Henrietta in a bureaucratic, regimented environment with most of her self-determination denied. Then he said in a strong voice, "Well, you'll need an excuse other than Daisy dying to take your mother away . . . for Daisy is going to live a very long time."

Then the intense vigil began, all the doctoring and care and prayer. But something extraordinary happened. By word of mouth, Cornelius learned of Henrietta's fate, and small amounts of money began coming in to pay a bill the doctor never intended to send. Prayer candles were lit at altars. And Sunday mornings the veterinarian left his family and the horses he loves and the springer spaniels he walks with in the fields and went to Daisy's kennel; scootched down to sit on the concrete kennel run; and with love and a beseeching voice, hand-fed her.

You're right. It took a long time, but Daisy lived, and Henrietta kissed her daughter good-bye. The following week, Cornelius saw the sun shine again. For down the walk came Henrietta and the little white fluff named Daisy.

A vet hadn't just saved a dog, he'd saved a woman as well and lifted the spirits of his community For Cornelius—with all that Oregon rain—would still have that ray of sunshine named Henrietta come passing by, propelled by a little white dog called Daisy.

—*Bill Tarrant*

Captain's Log

The fish and game officer gasped in surprise as he knelt beside the wounded "deer" he had been sent to rescue. He was responding to a call from an elderly woman who lived across from the vacant lot where she had spotted the animal in distress.

It was not a deer, however, but a blue Doberman with a coat color similar to that of the deer frequenting the area. But she was right on one score. The young male dog was, indeed, in distress. He had been starved sufficiently for his ribs to stand out with razor sharpness, leaving him half his proper weight. Bruises and sores covered his body, and his left eye had been put out, perhaps by a bullet, the officer guessed. He gathered the limp, unresisting body up in his arms and headed for the local humane shelter. The young dog was close to breathing his last, and he shivered and cowered in terror when he heard all the barking and commotion at the shelter.

Doberman rescue was one of my specialties. I owned a small herd of dairy goats and had used their nutritious milk to nurse back to health many orphaned and ill animals over the years. And so I received the S.O.S. call that was to lead to one of the most rewarding relationships of my life.

We called him Captain because he was so obviously *not* in command of his ship at this moment in his life.

Molly, my black Labrador, was only mildly interested in such an almost inanimate object that smelled like a dog, but refused to respond to any of her advances or invitations to play. When she discovered how much of my time Captain was to occupy, Molly pouted and shunned us both for several weeks.

Captain had been starved for a long enough time that his digestive system had trouble handling much beyond mere tablespoonfuls of food fed every two to three hours around the clock.

It was a good thing I am a light sleeper. It was much like a new mother with her first baby, hearing every sound and movement and up like a flash to minister to his every need, day or night.

The plan was to rehabilitate him and find him a new home. But long after his physical scars had healed, his mental and emotional wounds still left him too vulnerable to place. Every time a hand was raised above shoulder level, he dropped to the ground in fear. Yard work that involved shovels, hoes, rakes, even brooms sent him off to a safe corner. What unbelievable abuse must have been heaped on what was proving to be a very soft, gentle temperament.

He and Molly had finally become good friends. Molly loved bossing him around, reminding him that she was top dog. But I began to notice that more and more often Cap was able to con Molly into doing things his way. He was beginning to exercise the passive-dominant techniques he would develop to perfection and eventually use to charm all who were to know him.

After working with him for over a year, I began to despair of ever successfully rehabilitating him. He sensed my frustration, for he stretched across my feet, rested his chin on my leg, and looked up at me with such an intense look of love, hope, and promise that I knew at that moment he was going to live with us to the end of his time.

He must have telepathically received the message, because from that day on he really blossomed. A great "talker," he assumed that position at my feet, head on my knee, several times a day. We held conversations about everything from the day's events to my long-range plans for the future. He mouthed answers at appropriate pauses, dearly loving those sessions, that one eye locked into mine, trying so hard to comprehend. Animals are creatures of habit, and that was the beginning of a daily ritual to be treasured by us.

The anxious, fearful look was gradually replaced by one of serenity and trust, with a hint of the puckish sense of humor resting just below the surface. He was now ready for some socialization. Captain was the consummate host in his own home, making everyone glad they had come to visit us. Now, as long as I was within sight, he surprised me by enjoying and reaching out to people he met in the park and on the street.

Our kennel club made monthly visits to area nursing homes. Since he was a gentle, slow-moving dog with a slick coat that felt like the finest satin, great for petting, we let him join the group on a trial run. He was an unparalleled success and spent the next ten years sharing all the love and compassion his great heart could muster with those old folks he felt such a need to comfort.

The Arizona Veterinary Medical Association gives annual awards to outstanding animals in the state. Captain was nominated by several nursing-home directors for special recognition. The bronze plaque was presented at the time of their combined meeting with the American Veterinary Medical Association, making it a nationwide audience.

Captain was groomed and scrubbed until every inch of him shone. He knew it was his day, and his stub of a tail was in perpetual motion. We were told to stand on the floor in front of the stage to receive the award, while the speaker and microphone were up on the stage above us. Cap was sure he could not be seen at floor level, so, on his own, he jumped up on the stage, went right out to the edge and gave that huge crowd his "Most Happy Fella" grin. His tail was a blur in response to the thunderous applause. What a ham!

On the way home Cap got his favorite treat—a Big Mac, no ketchup.

The kennel club also gave programs every year at the elementary schools, stressing responsible dog ownership. It was hoped that if we could influence children at a young enough age, good habits might follow through into adulthood.

Even though he had been badly abused, I never saw Cap react to a perceived threat with a lifted lip or growl. He seemed always willing to turn the other cheek. And so, it followed that he joined the school brigade. After our program we allowed the children to come up and pet and handle the dogs, so we had to be certain we used only solid dogs able to cope with any surprise a young child might throw their way.

As I saw him surrounded by hugging, patting, grabbing youngsters, his head rose above them all with one of his characteristic ear-to-ear grins. I should not have worried. His next chapter was ready to be written. He accumulated several large manila envelopes full of thank-yous from the hundreds of children he captivated over the years.

Hollywood came to our town to shoot a film using the local scenery as backdrop. There was a part for a dog. About a dozen hopefuls showed up for the audition. Cap and I were late. As I hurriedly dragged him down the street, he greeted everyone we passed, finally stopping to have a brief chat with the policeman directing traffic. The director and the lead actor, Peter Coyote, were watching our approach, and they made their decision right then and there. Cap had the part.

He was trained to the silent whistle and he would howl on command, so he did possess some workable talent.

It was a CBS movie, *Living a Lie*, with Jill Eikenberry of *LA Law*. Cap portrayed the dog of a bad guy who leaves him in his truck while he goes into a saloon for hours. Cap's costume was a blue-and-pink bandanna and his stage was the back of a pickup.

On the night his scene was shot, he performed flawlessly and received "gold pay"—$150 for eight hours' work. That was double the going rate, his reward for getting it right the first time with no need for retakes.

Poor Cap. He was a hit, all right, but sick as the proverbial dog for three days after the shoot. While waiting for his scene, he was enticing all the sweet young things in the cast to feed him pieces of rolled-up turkey, roast beef, and cheese from the chuckwagon buffet.

When he passed ten, I began to limit some of his outside activities. He had some new duties at home. My mother, who was in her terminal years, came to live with us. He appointed himself her personal nurse and bodyguard; she was never left alone. He gave her all the best care and courtesy he had been exercising over the years, rooting his head under her hand when she was too weak to lift it, remaining motionless for hours so she could touch and feel him.

After my mother died, Cap turned his attentions to the two new Manchester terrier puppies that had just been born in the walk-in closet in my bedroom. Their mother, Tracy, was a holy terror about anybody coming near her babies, but Captain worked his usual magic and soon had them snuggling up with him for their naps and chewing their rubber toys together, while Tracy placidly sat by and watched, enjoying the services of her live-in nanny.

When he was thirteen, we moved to a five-acre mini-ranch in the foothills of the Rockies. We visited the local nursing home and veterans' home, but Captain's stamina was beginning to fail, and he seemed to prefer staying home. He made a daily inspection tour of the five acres and liked best to lie out front watching the deer and antelope that grazed in our pasture. They dashed off when any other dogs were spotted, but soon learned to trust and ignore Captain. Perhaps the deer thought he was one of them, just as he was mistakenly identified so many years ago.

In the backyard was a children's playhouse built over a sandbox. That sandbox became Cap's summer castle, where he burrowed down into the cool sand for his afternoon naps.

No matter how far he had managed to come, there was still a remnant of insecurity he had to deal with. Every night he took a square of soft flannel to bed with him. Tucked between his crossed front feet, he pulled up a good piece of it, "talked" to it for a few minutes, and then fell asleep sucking on it. Had he lost his mother at too young an age? Every night he had a fresh "comfort rag" or "Linus blanket," so the weekly wash always had its small pile of flannel squares with holes chewed in them.

The spring he was fifteen, he developed a slight pink discharge from one nostril. Antibiotics and steroids took care of it for a time, but it returned, and we were forced to consider a nasal bone tumor. They are usually slow-growing. By the time symptoms appear, it is too late to do much. There did not seem to be any pain, only a degree of annoyance. He ate all his meals with his usual gusto, chewed on his toys, and napped with the Manchesters, who doted on him. But one Sunday morning he ran to me with blood pouring from his nostril. The look in his eye was the same as the very first day I saw him—not pain, but fear. He didn't know what was happening to him, and he was pleading with me to help him, because he was scared.

In one of our conversations during that first year we shared, I promised him I would never make him suffer any more pain than was absolutely necessary, because he had already endured more than his share. Today was the day I was being called on to make good on that promise.

A quick call was made to the vet. If she hurried, she'd be at the house in twenty minutes. I cradled him in my arms, and we had our last conversation. He never took his eye off mine, not even when the vet arrived, put on the tourniquet, and administered the shot that sent him to the Rainbow Bridge to wait for me. He could no longer talk, but the message in his eye was clearly one of "Thank you and good-bye."

His comfort rags sit on a shelf in the laundry room. Captain doesn't need them anymore, so he left them for us in case we are in need of the consolation he can no longer personally give to us. The Manchesters still check the sandbox every day and walk the property line in his place. They don't have much interest in their toys or know quite where to go for their naps. They will eventually work out of it, but I think a part of them will always wonder and remember the friend they loved so dearly.

Is this an American rags-to-riches saga or a love story? Perhaps it's a bit of both. But I think the most meaningful highlights of this journey surround the hundreds of people irresistibly touched by that big infectious grin and perpetually wagging tail stub, and the loving heart of a dog who returned the best he had to give in answer to the worst humankind had offered him.

Angels are big this year. Perhaps God does occasionally send one of His special emissaries to earth to show us the real power of His love. And just perhaps I was touched by an angel—a four-legged one named Captain.

—*Bonnie J. Keith*

CHAPTER FIVE

Funny Bones

I am joy in a woolly coat, come to dance into your life to make you laugh!

—Julie Church

Dogs laugh, but they laugh with their tails.

—Max Eastman

He knew so many words that my husband and I took to spelling in front of him. Of course, always being treated as a person (he often sat at the table with a napkin around his neck) Fafner considered himself a person. His attitude toward other dogs was a mixture of arrogance and contempt, and he barked furiously whenever he saw one.

—Brooke Astor

Jeremy Boob, Golden Retriever

One summer, we were living in the country and that, along with our generally relaxed attitude toward kids and animals, created a tidal wave. There were Winnie, Biddy, Nel, and Oomiac, respectively a pug, toy poodle, random-bred dog (or mutt), and Siberian husky. That was when our daughter, Pamela, decided her first week's paycheck from her new job as a riding teacher could best be spent on . . . you guessed it, a dog. That was how we got Jeremy Boob, the golden retriever.

I must confess, Pamela handled it like a pro. I was at this very typewriter when my study door flew open. Pamela entered carrying a huge golden puppy and was followed by several of her friends. The plan, apparently, was that they would all stare me down if I got tough. It is very difficult to be hardheaded with half the youth in town staring at you. Anyway, Jeremy stayed and is a wonderful dog.

Jeremy came from a good old line—massive head, broad chest, lovely, absolutely saintlike disposition. His father, Junior Grossman, was just like him and appears to have sired half the goldens east of Hawaii.

Jeremy, alas, has the very bad habit of escaping from the fenced yard where most of our dogs are kept. When free, Jeremy heads for a special bus stop he knows where the school bus unloads a parcel of kids every afternoon at just about the same time. Jeremy, enjoying his temporary freedom, visits with the kids and picks his kid-for-the-day and follows him or her home. He usually scrounges a cookie or two—so the rumors that have drifted back to us suggest—and after a bit asks to be let out and heads home. Although there is very little traffic in our area, we do discourage roaming.

Jeremy wears a tag on his collar, of course, with our name and phone number and his name as well. On one of Jeremy's expeditions into other homes, other kitchens, the thoughtful mother of the child he had selected for the day felt the dog should not be turned loose. Checking the tag of the exceedingly agreeable Jeremy, she found it had rusted somewhat and only Jeremy's last name, Boob, survived.

The phone call about Jeremy came and was taken by my exceptionally English mother-in-law.

The voice on the other end was very clear: "I have your Boob."

"I beg your pardon!" my mother-in-law answered. You have never heard what those four words can sound like until they have been delivered by Phyllis Langdon Smith Barclay, who graduated from Mrs. Whatchamacallit's School for the Daughters of Gentlemen in Henley-on-Thames. "You have my what?"

"I have your Boob."

My son was dispatched immediately by his nana to collect his sister's dog, while I fixed my mother-in-law a glass of sherry. "Whatever do you suppose possessed that woman! My boob indeed."

—Roger Caras

Making a Point

My partner in the radio business, Jimmy Joe Woodard, loved dogs. Especially bird dogs. Joe was known for having the best bird dogs in our part of the country. One of his very best was ol' Jake. For his birthday one year, Joe's wife hired a photographer to produce a portrait of Jake in point. It was a large, beautiful picture, and Joe placed it on the most prominent wall in his spacious office.

Like people, dogs respond to care and attention. Joe fed 'em, played with 'em, trained 'em, worked 'em, and even took 'em swimming. He'd had dozens of 'em. And over the years, two of his favorites were a pair of pointers named Dot and Zell.

He loved 'em, so when Dot's hips were ruined by arthritis, he spent a handsome sum of money on hip replacement surgery for her.

Of course, a bird dog's job is to point birds, and the good ones live to do it and love to do it, just like the people who are good at what they do. When they spot birds, they lock into a point. And, if they spot another dog in point, they back the other dog by freezing in position and point the other dog. It's a real picture of how teamwork is supposed to be.

After Dot's hips were replaced, her hunting days were over. She became Joe's beloved pet. He'd ride her around with him in his truck during his off time, and she'd follow him wherever he would go.

The first time he brought her to the office, she padded down the hall after him. As she rounded the corner into his office she spotted that portrait of Jake. Dot locked into a magnificent point, right there in the radio station! She was still backing up ol' Jake!

—*Bryan Townsend*

Puss and the Boot

In 1987 we moved into an old farmhouse (circa 1790). There were just the four of us: my husband, me, our daughter, and Pepper, our springer spaniel.

We were only getting settled in when I saw evidence of mice. Since I don't like the dangers of poisoning, baits, traps, or the sticky stuff that the mice can't climb off, I decided I needed a cat.

We got Puss Puss, a tiny little red kitten.

As time passed he turned out to be a wonderful, sweet, fun-filled, spoiled kitten. We all loved him except Pepper, who was *extremely* jealous.

Then our problems began. We were keeping Puss Puss inside because he was so tiny, yet every time our backs were turned—he was outside. How he got there was completely perplexing. What was going on?

Finally one day we saw Pepper opening the back door with his nose just a few inches and letting the kitten out and with a look of pure innocence returning to his business of being number one pet.

—Joan Stauffer

Emergency Rover

Steve Ford of Owensboro, Kentucky, was in a panic. He'd heard his beloved Labrador retriever had been in a traffic accident, but he couldn't find the dog anywhere. Finally he called Audubon Animal Hospital and found out that his dog, JoJo, was already there.

After injuring his paw in the accident, JoJo ran about a mile to the animal hospital, where he is an occasional boarder, and admitted himself. "He just came to the door and he stopped and he held up his injured paw," said veterinarian Robert Byrd.

JoJo was not required to fill out any forms for treatment.

"He came down without his owner's permission," Byrd said, "and not being properly admitted by the owner, I didn't know whether to care for him or not. But I'm sure JoJo has his own checking account."

In a couple of days, JoJo was treated and released to Steve Ford.

—Michael Capuzzo

Ralph, the Basset Hound

Ralph was a large brown-and-white male, who weighed about eighty-five pounds. My favorite story about him is when he would lie down beside the road and sleep. (He could sleep anywhere, no matter what was going on.) People walking by would see him and come over to look. (He didn't sleep in a curled-up position but lay stretched out on his side, looking a lot like a dead pig.) When they reached down to pet him, he wouldn't move, or else he'd kind of groan and look up at them with his bloodshot eyes. Most people would decide that he was hit by a car and would come up to the house to tell us what had happened. The first time I was really worried, but I started having my doubts after asking the people if they actually saw him get hit. They'd say, "No, but he just lays there and groans and doesn't move." I'd walk out to him and reach down to pet him, and say, "Ralph, this is really embarrassing, get up and come home." I thanked the people, and then Ralph would get up and trot along after me. This happened several times. At our local pet parade, there was a category for "Laziest Dog," where a small amount of prize money could be won. Ralph won easily for two years in a row, before he passed away.

—Carl Hanson

The Answer

Many years ago, before I had developed an interest in animal behavior, I was working in a busy practice in Glasgow, Scotland. One evening a man came into the consulting room with a Jack Russell terrier under his arm and tears in his eyes. He shook his head slowly. "I'm afraid I'm going to have to ask you to put her to sleep, Doctor," he said sadly as he gently laid the dog on the exam table.

"What seems to be the problem?" I asked.

"Well, Sally here is very destructive. She attacks and eats the phone whenever it rings. She has destroyed three phones so far, and we just can't afford to keep replacing them."

"She eats phones?" I asked incredulously. "Can't you just put the phone out of the way?"

"No, I'm afraid not. She finds it wherever you put it. I love her very much and I haven't come to this decision lightly, but it looks as if we'll just have to put her to sleep."

I looked at Sally, who cocked her head slightly and looked back at me silently. She was a pretty dog and in her prime. It seemed such a pity to put her to sleep.

"Could I have one go at treating her?" I asked, dredging my memory for a solution to this problem.

"What would you do, Doctor?" the man asked.

"I could try putting her on Valium," I suggested as a long shot. "Maybe that would calm her down a little."

"All right," said the man. "It certainly seems to be worth a try."

I prescribed a relatively low dose of Valium to be given three times a day and sent the man home with his dog. The following week the man appeared again. He looked even sadder than before.

"It didn't work, Doctor," he said. "She has gone after the phones again. I'm afraid you're just going to have to put her to sleep."

"The dose I used was fairly conservative," I said. "Couldn't you give me another week and we'll try a higher dose?"

He agreed and set off again for another week at double the dose. The following week it was the same story—no improvement—and I knew I was running out of time. I pleaded for one last week at the maximum dose, and he agreed somewhat reluctantly to this final measure. When he finally returned after what seemed like an exceptionally long week, he was beaming from ear to ear.

"She's all right now, Doctor," he said. "I think we can keep her. Your medicine worked."

I was delighted at the good news and said to him, "So am I to understand she doesn't pay any attention to the phone at all now?"

"Well, no, that's not quite true," he said. "She still does try to get to it, but now she moves so slowly that I can catch her before she gets there."

—Dr. Nicholas Dodman

Training Zippy

Everybody should have a pet. And I'm not saying this just because the American Pet Council gave me a helicopter. I'm saying it because my family has always owned pets, and without them, our lives would not be nearly so rich in—call me sentimental, but this is how I feel—dirt.

Pets are nature's way of reminding us that, in the incredibly complex ecological chain of life, there is no room for furniture. For example, the only really nice furnishing I own is an Oriental rug that I bought, with the help of a decorator, in a failed attempt to become tasteful. This rug is way too nice for an onion-dip–intensive household like mine, and I seriously thought about keeping it in a large safe-deposit box; but I finally decided, in a moment of abandon, to put it on the floor. I then conducted a comprehensive rug-behavior training seminar for our main dog, Earnest, and our small auxiliary dog, Zippy.

"*No!*" I told them approximately seventy-five times while looking very stern and pointing at the rug. This proven training technique caused them to slink around the way dogs do when they feel tremendously guilty but have no idea why. Satisfied, I went out to dinner.

I later figured out, using an electronic calculator, that this rug covers approximately 2 percent of the total square footage of my house, which means that if you (not you personally) were to have a random diarrhea attack in my home, the odds are approximately forty-nine to one against your having it on my Oriental rug. The odds against your having four random attacks on this rug are more than five million to one. So I had to conclude that it was done on purpose. The rug appeared to have been visited by a group of specially bred, highly trained Doberman poopers; but I determined, by interrogating both dogs, that the entire massive output was the work of Zippy. Probably he was trying to do the right thing. Probably, somewhere in the Cocoa Puff–sized nodule of nerve tissue that serves as his brain, he dimly remembered that The Master had told him something about the rug. Yes! That's it! To the rug!

At least Zippy had the decency to feel bad about what he did, which is more than you can say for Mousse, a dog that belonged to a couple named Mike and Sandy. Mousse was a Labrador retriever, which is a large, enthusiastic, bulletproof species of dog made entirely from synthetic materials. This is the kind of dog that, if it takes an interest in your personal regions (which of course it does), you cannot fend it off with a blowtorch.

So anyway, Mike and Sandy had two visitors who wore expensive, brand-new down-filled parkas, which somehow got left for several hours in a closed room with Mousse. When the door was finally opened, the visibility in the room had been drastically reduced by a raging down storm, at the center of which was a large quivering down clot, looking like a huge mutant duckling, except that it had Mousse's radiantly happy eyes.

For several moments Mike and Sandy and their guests stared at this apparition, then Mike, a big, strong, highly authoritative guy, strode angrily into the room and slammed the door. He was in there for several minutes, then emerged, looking very serious. The down clot stood behind him, wagging its tail cheerfully.

"I talked to Mousse," Mike said, "and he says he didn't do it."

People often become deranged by pets. Derangement is the only possible explanation for owning a cat, an animal whose preferred mode of communication is to sink its claws three-quarters of an inch into your flesh. God help the cat owner who runs out of food. It's not uncommon to see an elderly woman sprinting through the supermarket with one or more cats clinging, leech-like, to her leg as she tries desperately to reach the pet-food section before collapsing from blood loss.

Of course, for sheer hostility in a pet, you can't beat a parrot. I base this statement on a parrot I knew named Charles who belonged to a couple named Ed and Ginny. Charles had an IQ of 260 and figured out early in life that if he talked to people, they'd get close enough so he could bite them. He especially liked to bite Ed, whom Charles wanted to drive out of the mar-riage so he could have Ginny, the house, the American Express card, etc. So in an effort to improve their rela-tionship, Ginny hatched (ha ha!) this plan wherein Ed took Charles to—I am not making this up—Parrot Obedience School. Every Saturday morning, Ed and Charles would head off to receive expert training, and every Saturday afternoon Ed would come home with chunks missing from his arm. Eventually Ginny real-ized that it was never going to work, so she got rid of Ed.

I'm just kidding, of course. Nobody would take Ed. Ginny got rid of Charles, who now works as a public-relations advisor to Miss Zsa Zsa Gabor. So we see that there are many pluses to having an animal friend, which is why you should definitely buy a pet. If you act right now, I'll also give you a heck of a deal on a rug.

—*Dave Barry*

The Lobster Apso

One holiday last year, my husband and I decided to cook live Maine lobster, a real treat for both of us. Our Lhasa apso, Bear, is very inquisitive and intelligent, and we wondered how he would react to a live lobster in the house. We purchased the lobsters and brought them home. Bear is the kind of dog that seems to love all animals and children so we figured it would be fine.

Our kitchen has two entrances, so we placed one of the lobsters on the floor. Bear came forward and stared down at the crusty obstacle for a short time. Slowly pacing forward and back, trying to decide what was going on, he went around to the other entrance in the kitchen, which brought him to the back side of the lobster. He smelled it from behind, trying to figure it out.

He suddenly left the kitchen and went to his toy box, grabbing a tennis ball. Bear brought the tennis ball to his new friend and dropped it in front of the lobster. Thinking the lobster would play, he waited for a response for a while, waiting for the lobster to throw it back.

It was so cute, their interaction, I could not cook the lobster realizing the communication going on between the two. Dinner went on hold, and we have not been able to consume a lobster since.

—Linda and George Lafferty

Travels with Lucy

When she sees me packing, my white miniature poodle, Lucy, crawls into her travel crate and stares out at me with big brown eyes. It's her way of telling me she doesn't want to be left behind.

She shouldn't worry. In her seven years she's accompanied me on many trips. There are towns in Greece, Turkey, Syria, and Indonesia where everybody knows her name. Women point, children giggle, and great mustachioed men call, "Oh, Loo-see," sounding like Ricky Ricardo. I don't merit such attention; I'm just her owner.

Traveling with a dog is not an inconspicuous way to go. In Muslim countries, people told me, a dog wouldn't be welcome, because dogs are considered unclean. Nothing could have been further from the truth. Lucy was my ambassadress, a curly-haired, four-legged symbol of goodwill. Ferryboat captains, bus drivers, and hoteliers made extra room for us. Waiters saved her tidbits. Sometimes the attention was overwhelming.

Poodles are a great rarity in Indonesia, and as usual Lucy was popular. People would say, *"Bagus, bagus,"* in tones of admiration, extending a cautious hand, but they rarely touched her. They liked to watch her, though.

In Yogyjakarta, a hot and historic town in central Java, I took advantage of the hotel pool for an evening dip. Lucy followed me from one end of the pool to the other, worried that I might somehow manage to escape her watchful eye. After several minutes she must have decided it was too hot for running. She launched herself into the water with a flying leap and started to swim laps with me. I hauled her out of the pool and scolded her, aware of half-seen faces scrutinizing us from behind the shrubbery. Someone tittered.

Next morning, the woman at the front desk asked, "Was that your dog swimming in the pool last night?" With a sinking heart I confessed that it was.

"Please let her do it again. I didn't get to see."

—*Diana Kordas*

Bow Vows

In a ceremony accompanied by howls both from the betrothed and from their invited guests, Maximillian Von Pershing, fourteen, and Coco La Moco, fifteen—a tan, gray, and white mutt described as "ten percent poodle"—were pronounced dachshund and wife.

The groom wore a black tuxedo and top hat. He was escorted on a purple leash by the best man. The bride wore a white lace bow in her hair and a veil over her back. Her leash was trimmed with lace. The newlyweds exchanged "woofs," sealed their bond with dog biscuits, and exchanged vows read by a member of the wedding, which went off smoothly except for the German shepherd barking from the bow of the boat that passed the gazebo. ("A jealous ex-lover," remarked someone in the crowd.)

The *St. Petersburg Times* carried excerpts from the wedding ceremony of Maximillian Von Pershing and Coco La Moco:

Dearly beloved
We are joined here together
To put these two lovers
On a firm legal tether
In an era and time
When divorce and infidelity abound
It's refreshing to find
This true noble hound
And you, Coco La Moco
Oh, 10 percent poodle
Have pledged to be true
Full kit and caboodle
So this union, one could say
In heaven was meant
I knew it the moment
Maxie picked up her scent.

—*Charles Hoskinson*

Cedric

The voice at the other end of the phone was oddly hesitant.

"Mr. Herriot . . . I should be grateful if you would come and see my dog." It was a woman, obviously upper-class.

"Certainly. What's the trouble?"

"Well . . . he . . . er . . . he seems to suffer from . . . a certain amount of flatus."

"I beg your pardon?"

There was a long pause. "He has . . . excessive flatus."

"In what way, exactly?"

"Well . . . I suppose you'd describe it as . . . windiness." The voice had begun to tremble.

I thought I could see a gleam of light. "You mean his stomach?"

"No, not his stomach. He passes . . . er . . . a considerable quantity of . . . wind from his . . . his . . ." A note of desperation had crept in.

"Ah, yes!" All became suddenly clear. "I quite understand. But that doesn't sound very serious. Is he ill?"

"No, he's very fit in other ways."

"Well, then, do you think it's necessary for me to see him?"

"Oh yes, indeed, Mr. Herriot. I wish you would come as soon as possible. It has become . . . quite a problem."

"All right," I said. "I'll look in this morning. Can I have your name and address, please?"

"It's Mrs. Rumney, The Laurels."

. . .

The Laurels was a very nice house on the edge of the town standing back from the road in a large garden. Mrs. Rumney herself let me in and I felt a shock of surprise at my first sight of her. It wasn't just that she was strikingly beautiful; there was an unworldly air about her. She would be around forty but had the appearance of a heroine in a Victorian novel—tall, willowy, ethereal. And I could understand immediately her hesitation on the phone. Everything about her suggested fastidiousness and delicacy.

"Cedric is in the kitchen," she said. "I'll take you through."

I had another surprise when I saw Cedric. An enormous boxer hurled himself on me in delight, clawing at my chest with the biggest, horniest feet I had seen for a long time. I tried to fight him off but he kept at me, panting ecstatically into my face and wagging his entire rear end.

"Sit down, boy!" the lady said sharply, then, as Cedric took absolutely no notice, she turned to me nervously. "He's so friendly."

"Yes," I said breathlessly, "I can see that." I finally managed to push the huge animal away and backed into a corner for safety. "How often does this . . . excessive flatus occur?"

As if in reply an almost palpable sulphurous wave arose from the dog and eddied around me. It appeared that the excitement of seeing me had activated Cedric's weakness. I was up against the wall and unable to obey my first instinct to run for cover so I held my hand over my face for a few moments before speaking.

Mrs. Rumney waved a lace handkerchief under her nose and the faintest flush crept into the pallor of her cheeks.

"Yes," she replied almost inaudibly. "Yes . . . that is it."

"Oh well," I said briskly, "there's nothing to worry about. Let's go into the other room and we'll have a word about his diet and a few other things."

It turned out that Cedric was getting rather a lot of meat, and I drew up a little chart cutting down the protein and adding extra carbohydrates. I prescribed a kaolin antacid mixture to be given night and morning and left the house in a confident frame of mind.

It was one of those trivial things, and I had entirely forgotten it when Mrs. Rumney phoned again.

"I'm afraid Cedric is no better, Mr. Herriot."

"Oh, I'm sorry to hear that. He's . . . er . . . still . . . yes . . . yes . . ." I spent a few moments in thought.

"I tell you what—I don't think I can do any more by seeing him at the moment, but I think you should cut out his meat completely for a week or two. Keep him on biscuits and brown bread rusked in the oven. Try him with that and vegetables, and I'll give you some powder to mix in his food. Perhaps you'd call round for it."

The powder was a pretty strong absorbent mixture and I felt sure it would do the trick, but a week later Mrs. Rumney was on the phone again.

"There's absolutely no improvement, Mr. Herriot." The tremble was back in her voice. "I . . . I do wish you'd come and see him again."

I couldn't see much point in viewing this perfectly healthy animal again but I promised to call. I had a busy day and it was after six o'clock before I got round to The Laurels. There were several cars in the drive and when I went into the house I saw that Mrs. Rumney had a few people in for drinks; people like herself—

upper-class and of obvious refinement. In fact, I felt rather a lout in my working clothes among the elegant gathering.

Mrs. Rumney was about to lead me through to the kitchen, when the door burst open and Cedric bounded delightedly into the midst of the company. Within seconds an aesthetic-looking gentleman was frantically beating off the attack as the great feet ripped down his waistcoat. He got away at the cost of a couple of buttons and the boxer turned his attention to one of the ladies. She was in imminent danger of losing her dress when I pulled the dog off her.

Pandemonium broke out in the graceful room. The hostess's plaintive appeals rang out above the cries of alarm as the big dog charged around, but very soon I realised that a more insidious element had crept into the situation. The atmosphere in the room became rapidly charged with an unmistakable effluvium, and it was clear that Cedric's unfortunate malady had reasserted itself.

I did my best to shepherd the animal out of the room but he didn't seem to know the meaning of obedience, and I chased him in vain. And as the embarrassing minutes ticked away I began to realise for the first time the enormity of the problem which confronted Mrs. Rumney. Most dogs break wind occasionally but Cedric was different: he did it all the time. And while his silent emanations were perhaps more treacherous, there was no doubt that the audible ones were painfully distressing in company like this.

Cedric made it worse, because at each rasping expulsion he would look round enquiringly at his back end, then gambol about the room as though the fugitive zephyr was clearly visible to him and he was determined to corner it.

It seemed a year before I got him out of there. Mrs. Rumney held the door wide as I finally managed to steer him towards it, but the big dog wasn't finished yet. On his way out he cocked a leg swiftly and directed a powerful jet against an immaculate trouser leg.

I consulted my colleague Siegfried on the problem, and he suggested a diet of charcoal biscuits. Cedric ate them in vast quantities and with evident enjoyment but they, like everything else, made not the slightest difference to his condition.

And all the time I pondered upon the enigma of Mrs. Rumney. She had lived in Darrowby for several years but the townsfolk knew little about her. It was a matter of debate whether she was a widow or separated from her husband. But I was not interested in such things; the biggest mystery to me was how she ever got involved with a dog like Cedric.

It was difficult to think of any animal less suited to her personality. Apart from his regrettable affliction he was in every way the opposite to herself; a great thick-headed rambunctious extrovert totally out of place in her gracious ménage. I never did find out how they came together but on my visits I found that Cedric had one admirer at least.

He was Con Fenton, a retired farm worker who did a bit of jobbing gardening and spent an average of three days a week at The Laurels. The boxer romped down the drive after me as I was leaving and the old man looked at him with undisguised admiration.

"By gaw," he said, "he's a fine dog, is that!"

"Yes, he is, Con, he's a good chap, really." And I meant it. You couldn't help liking Cedric when you got to know him. He was utterly amiable and without vice, and he gave off a constant aura not merely of noxious vapours but of bonhomie. When he tore off people's buttons or sprinkled their trousers he did it in a spirit of the purest amity.

"Just look at them limbs!" breathed Con, staring rapturously at the dog's muscular thighs. "By heck, 'e can jump ower that gate as if it weren't there. He's what ah call a dog!"

As he spoke it struck me that Cedric would be likely to appeal to him because he was very like the boxer himself: not overburdened with brains, built like an ox with powerful shoulders and a big constantly grinning face—they were two of a kind.

"Aye, ah allus likes it when t'missus lets him out in t'garden," Con went on. He always spoke in a peculiar snuffling manner. "He's grand company."

I looked at him narrowly. No, he wouldn't be likely to notice Cedric's complaint since he always saw him out of doors.

On my way back to the surgery I brooded on the fact that I was achieving absolutely nothing with my treatment. And though it seemed ridiculous to worry about a case like this, there was no doubt the thing had begun to prey on my mind. In fact I began to transmit my anxieties to Siegfried. As I got out of the car he was coming down the steps of Skeldale House and he put a hand on my arm.

"You've been to The Laurels, James? Tell me," he enquired solicitously, "how is your farting boxer today?"

"Still at it, I'm afraid," I replied, and my colleague shook his head in commiseration.

We were both defeated. Maybe if chlorophyll tablets had been available in those days they might have helped, but as it was I had tried everything. It seemed certain that nothing would alter the situation. And it wouldn't have been so bad if the owner had been anybody else but Mrs. Rumney; I found that even discussing the thing with her had become almost unbearable.

Siegfried's student brother, Tristan, didn't help, either. When seeing practice he was very selective in the cases he wished to observe, but he was immediately attracted to Cedric's symptoms and insisted on coming with me on one occasion. I never took him again because as we went in the big dog bounded from his mistress's side and produced a particularly sonorous blast as if in greeting.

Tristan immediately threw out a hand in a dramatic gesture and declaimed: "Speak on, sweet lips that never told a lie!" That was his only visit. I had enough trouble without that.

I didn't know it at the time but a greater blow awaited me. A few days later Mrs. Rumney was on the phone again.

"Mr. Herriot, a friend of mine has such a sweet little boxer bitch. She wants to bring her along to be mated with Cedric."

"Eh?"

"She wants to mate her bitch with my dog."

"With Cedric . . . ?" I clutched at the edge of the desk. It couldn't be true! "And . . . and are you agreeable?"

"Yes, of course."

I shook my head to dispel the feeling of unreality. I found it incomprehensible that anyone should want to reproduce Cedric, and as I gaped into the receiver a frightening vision floated before me of eight little Cedrics all with his complaint. But, of course, such a thing wasn't hereditary. I took a grip of myself and cleared my throat.

"Very well, then, Mrs. Rumney, you'd better go ahead."

There was a pause. "But Mr. Herriot, I want you to supervise the mating."

"Oh really, I don't think that's necessary." I dug my nails into my palm. "I think you'll be all right without me."

"Oh, but I would be much happier if you were there. Please come," she said appealingly.

Instead of emitting a long-drawn groan I took a deep breath.

"Right," I said. "I'll be along in the morning."

All that evening I was obsessed by a feeling of dread. Another acutely embarrassing session was in store with this exquisite woman. Why was it I always had to share things like this with her? And I really feared the worst. Even the daftest dog, when confronted with a bitch in heat, knows instinctively how to proceed, but with a really ivory-skulled animal like Cedric I wondered . . .

And the next morning all my fears were realised. The bitch, Trudy, was a trim little creature and showed every sign of willingness to be cooperative. Cedric, on the other hand, though obviously delighted to meet her, gave no hint of doing his part. After sniffing her over, he danced around her a few times, goofy-faced, tongue lolling. Then he had a roll on the lawn before charging at her and coming to a full stop, big feet outsplayed, head down, ready to play. I sighed. It was as I thought. The big chump didn't know what to do.

This pantomime went on for some time and, inevitably, the emotional strain brought on a resurgence of his symptoms. Frequently he paused to inspect his tail as though he had never heard noises like that before.

He varied his dancing routine with occasional headlong gallops round the lawn, and it was after he had done about ten successive laps that he seemed to decide

he ought to do something about the bitch. I held my
breath as he approached her but unfortunately he chose
the wrong end to commence operations. Trudy had put
up with his nonsense with great patience but when she
found him busily working away in the region of her left
ear it was too much. With a shrill yelp she nipped him
in the hind leg and he shot away in alarm.

After that whenever he came near she warned him off
with bared teeth. Clearly she was disenchanted with her
bridegroom and I couldn't blame her.

"I think she's had enough, Mrs. Rumney," I said.

I certainly had had enough and so had the poor lady,
judging by her slight breathlessness, flushed cheeks and
waving handkerchief.

"Yes . . . yes . . . I suppose you're right," she replied.

So Trudy was taken home and that was the end of
Cedric's career as a stud dog.

This last episode decided me. I had to have a talk with
Mrs. Rumney and a few days later I called in at The
Laurels.

"Maybe you'll think it's none of my business," I said,
"but I honestly don't think Cedric is the dog for you. In
fact he's so wrong for you that he is upsetting your
life."

Mrs. Rumney's eyes widened. "Well . . . he is a
problem in some ways . . . but what do you suggest?"

"I think you should get another dog in his place.
Maybe a poodle or a corgi—something smaller, something you could control."

"But Mr. Herriot, I couldn't possibly have Cedric put
down." Her eyes filled quickly with tears. "I really am
fond of him despite . . . despite everything."

"No, no, of course not!" I said. "I like him too. He

has no malice in him. But I think I have a good idea. Why not let Con Fenton have him?"

"Con . . . ?"

"Yes, he admires Cedric tremendously and the big fellow would have a good life with the old man. He has a couple of fields behind his cottage and keeps a few beasts. Cedric could run to his heart's content out there and Con would be able to bring him along when he does the garden. You'd still see him three times a week."

Mrs. Rumney looked at me in silence for a few moments and I saw in her face the dawning of relief and hope.

"You know, Mr. Herriot, I think that could work very well. But are you sure Con would take him?"

"I'd like to bet on it. An old bachelor like him must be lonely. There's only one thing worries me. Normally they only meet outside, and I wonder how it would be when they were indoors and Cedric started to . . . when the old trouble—"

"Oh, I think that would be all right," Mrs. Rumney broke in quickly. "When I go on holiday Con always takes him for a week or two and he has never mentioned any . . . anything unusual . . . in that way."

I got up to go. "Well, that's fine. I should put it to the old man right away."

Mrs. Rumney rang within a few days. Con had jumped at the chance of taking on Cedric, and the pair had apparently settled in happily together. She had also taken my advice and acquired a poodle puppy.

I didn't see the new dog till it was nearly six months old and its mistress asked me to call to treat it for a slight attack of eczema. As I sat in the graceful room looking at Mrs. Rumney, cool, poised, tranquil, with the little white creature resting on her knee, I couldn't help feeling how right and fitting the whole scene was. The lush carpet, the trailing velvet curtains, the fragile tables with their load of expensive china and framed miniatures. It was no place for Cedric.

Con Fenton's cottage was less than half a mile away and on my way back to the surgery, on an impulse, I pulled up at the door. The old man answered my knock, and his big face split into a delighted grin when he saw me.

"Come in, young man!" he cried in his strange snuffy voice. "I'm right glad to see tha!"

I had hardly stepped into the tiny living room when a hairy form hurled itself upon me. Cedric hadn't changed a bit and I had to battle my way to the broken armchair by the fireside. Con settled down opposite and when the boxer leaped to lick his face he clumped him companionably on the head with his fist.

"Siddown, ye great daft bugger," he murmured with affection. Cedric sank happily onto the tattered hearth-rug at his feet and gazed up adoringly at his new master.

"Well, Mr. Herriot," Con went on as he cut up some villainous-looking plug tobacco and began to stuff it into his pipe. "I'm right grateful to ye for gettin' me this grand dog. By gaw, he's a topper and ah wouldn't sell 'im for any money. No man could ask for a better friend."

"Well, that's great, Con," I said. "And I can see that the big chap is really happy here."

The old man ignited his pipe and a cloud of acrid smoke rose to the low, blackened beams. "Aye, he's 'ardly ever inside. A gurt strong dog like 'im wants to work 'is energy off, like."

But just at that moment Cedric was obviously working something else off because the familiar pungency rose from him even above the billowings from the pipe. Con seemed oblivious of it, but in the enclosed space I found it overpowering.

"Ah well," I gasped. "I just looked in for a moment to see how you were getting on together. I must be on my way." I rose hurriedly and stumbled towards the door but the redolence followed me in a wave. As I passed the table with the remains of the old man's meal I saw what seemed to be the only form of ornament in the cottage, a cracked vase holding a magnificent bouquet of carnations. It was a way of escape and I buried my nose in their fragrance.

Con watched me approvingly. "Aye, they're lovely flowers, aren't they? T'missus at Laurels lets me bring 'ome what I want and I reckon them carnations is me favourite."

"Yes, they're a credit to you." I still kept my nose among the blooms.

"There's only one thing," the old man said pensively. "Ah don't get t'full benefit of 'em."

"How's that, Con?"

He pulled at his pipe a couple of times. "Well, you can hear ah speak a bit funny, like?"

"No . . . no . . . not really."

"Oh aye, ye know ah do. I've been like it since I were a lad. I 'ad a operation for adenoids and summat went wrong."

"Oh, I'm sorry to hear that," I said.

"Well, it's nowt serious, but it's left me lackin' in one way."

"You mean . . . ?" A light was beginning to dawn in my mind, an elucidation of how man and dog had found each other, of why their relationship was so perfect, of the certainty of their happy future together. It seemed like fate.

"Aye," the old man went on sadly. "I 'ave no sense of smell."

—*James Herriot*

CHAPTER SIX

Heroism

You do not think dogs will be in heaven? I tell you, they will be there long before any of us.
—Robert Louis Stevenson

The last great American heroes are dogs.
—Anonymous, 1988

The Leap of Love

One warm summer afternoon, Rae Anne Knitter and her fiancé Ray Thomas were out walking along the nature trails in the Cleveland Metroparks Rocky River Reservation. It's hard to find breathtaking natural scenery in a city, and Rae Anne and Ray, an amateur photographer, always liked to get away to the surprisingly rugged park. Rae Anne brought her dog, Woodie, a stubby little female collie mix who also loved the park.

In the middle of their hike, Ray wanted to capture the spectacular view from atop a steep shale cliff. Rae Anne waited on the path with her dog while Ray walked over the top of the hill and out of sight to position himself for the shot.

Suddenly, Woodie began twisting on her leash and tugging to escape from Rae Anne. "I knew something was wrong," Rae Anne said, "because Woodie is always so well behaved. She's never acted like that before." Rae Anne let go of Woodie's leash and followed her over the top of the hill. When she reached the brink she looked in horror at Ray lying facedown and unconscious in a stream eighty feet below. By Ray's side was Woodie.

Ray had lost his footing and plunged over the cliff. Woodie had seen Ray motionless at the bottom of the stream and taken the jump herself to help her friend. The dog had broken both her hips in the fall. Dragging her crushed hips along the ground, whimpering in pain, the dog struggled to Ray's side and nudged his face to keep it out of the water. When Ray, still unconscious, was breathing clear of the stream, Woodie hobbled toward the face of the cliff and began to bark frantically, calling for help.

Rae Anne rushed to call emergency medical technicians. Ray spent two months in the hospital, undergoing treatment for multiple fractures in his back and arm. Doctors concluded Woodie had saved him from drowning in the river. Woodie spent months recovering from internal injuries and broken bones. But after all her pain and suffering, Woodie underwent a personality change.

"She's more affectionate than ever," Rae Anne said.

—Teresa Banik Capuzzo

Patches

Marvin Scott, owner of a furniture store just south of Tacoma, Washington, came home from work at about 10:00 P.M. one bitter cold December night. The thermometer was hovering around zero, and the wind was whipping up waves on Lake Spanaway, where the Scotts' lakeside home sits.

Marvin was in his sixties, graying and bespectacled, given to dark suits, white shirts, and somber ties. But he was a square-shouldered, rugged man who liked to putter around his property, so he announced to his wife at almost 11:00 that night that he was going down to a small pier below their lake home to check on possible ice damage to a patrol boat moored there. As he clambered down the rocky, three-hundred-foot slope to the lake, Marvin was followed by his dog, Patches, a collie-malamute mix who liked to tag along.

At the lakeside, Marvin's fears were confirmed. Noting that a film of ice was beginning to form around the boat, Marvin picked up a timber and tried to push the stern line to crack the ice. But he did not realize that spray from the lake had made the pier boards glassy with ice, and as he pushed with the timber he slipped from the pier, his body struck a floating dock causing him to tear virtually all of the tendons and muscles in both legs, and he rolled off into the icy, fifteen-foot-deep water and went under. The freezing waters, roiled by the storm, began to pull him toward the middle of the lake.

Suddenly, while still below the surface, Marvin felt something grasp him by the hair. It was Patches, who had leaped into the icy waters and was holding his master firmly. Patches pulled the dazed and shivering man to the surface, then towed him nearly twenty feet to where he could seize the edge of the floating dock. Dimly aware that the dog, too, was by now nearly drowning and exhausted from his rescue efforts, Marvin managed to push him onto the dock.

But as Marvin, his legs immobile and useless, vainly attempted to climb onto the dock himself, the combination of the frigid water, his terrible injuries, and the water he had swallowed caused him to virtually black out, and his grip on the dock loosened. He fell back into the water and again went under.

But again it was Patches to the rescue. The courageous dog leaped in instantly, again seized him by the hair, and this time pulled him about four feet to the dock. After Marvin had recovered enough to push Patches onto the dock, the man hung on grimly to the dock and screamed for help. But with the late hour and the wind against him, his cries could not be heard. Marvin, his grip on the dock loosening once again, knew he had no more energy left to fight and despaired that he was going to die. As he began to slip into the water a third and final time, Patches braced his four feet firmly on the dock boards, grasped Marvin's overcoat collar in his teeth and tugged with might and main. Encouraged by this unexpected assistance, Marvin struggled with every ounce of strength he had left and somehow, between the two of them, the gasping man was able to pull his body up onto the dock.

After he had regained his breath, Marvin began crawling toward the house, with Patches in front of him holding tenaciously to his master's collar and using every bit of strength he possessed to help pull the shivering and agonized man along. Man and dog laboriously made their way in this fashion up the rock-studded, three-hundred-foot slope to a point near the back door, where Patches started barking a call for help, and Marvin was able to throw a stone against the door and alert his wife.

At Tacoma General Hospital, Marvin hovered between life and death for twenty-five days, with pneumonia a constant threat in addition to the massive operations required on both of his legs. Patches, exhausted but not hurt, recovered quickly. It was six months later, summer of the following year, before Marvin Scott was able to return to work at his furniture store. He needed two canes to get about, walking more deliberately now, so Patches slowed his gait to match the pace of his master when he tagged along on walks around the house by the lake.

—*Teresa Banik Capuzzo*

The Shepherd

This is a story from the Depression era that my aunt told on a number of occasions.

There is a small Canadian town across the Niagara River from Buffalo, New York. During the 1930s, my aunt and uncle lived in the town, as my uncle had found employment in Canada.

Both of them were animal lovers, and they owned two German shepherds at the time. My aunt was proudest of the female dog, Sissy.

They lived on a lovely, tree-lined avenue that sloped gently to the nearest cross street. On the corner of this intersection, there was a neighborhood store, where most of the residents did their shopping.

Farther up the hill from my aunt and uncle's house lived a disabled woman, Anna, who had to get around in a wheelchair.

Now and then, my aunt would let her dogs run loose, and on this one occasion, Anna was coming home with her purchases. It was the first time Sissy had seen Anna and her wheelchair. She ran up to her and placed both front paws on the arms of the chair and stared Anna in the face. Naturally, as helpless as she was, Anna was terrified.

Hearing her screams, my aunt ran over to them and called Sissy away. She apologized to Anna and was careful after that to make sure Anna was nowhere in sight when she let her dogs run.

This went on for quite a while, until one winter's evening. Now, remember that Ft. Erie, being just across the river from Buffalo, receives quite a lot of snow.

This evening, Anna was on her way home from the store, when her wheelchair got stuck in a snowdrift. Unable to free herself, she called for help, but no one heard her. No one, that is, but Sissy.

Out of the night, in a heavy snowstorm, she ran up to Anna. It was with mixed emotions that Anna saw Sissy run up to her. Too cold and miserable to protest, she watched in amazement as Sissy, with all her strength, tugged and pulled on the wheelchair, finally freeing it, and allowing Anna to get home safely.

After that, there was nothing too good for Sissy. Anna plied her with bones and other treats to show her appreciation.

—Elaine Cintorino

Scout's Honor

Only in the latter 1990s did the notion that animals have feelings and emotions begin to gain wide acceptance in academic circles in the United States. The authors and researchers who brought this news to the public need only have talked to Mary Gladys Baker of Waurika, Oklahoma, a decade before.

It was bitterly cold in Oklahoma that winter night in 1988, so cold Mary Gladys worried that her dogs, even in their comfortable doghouse, would suffer from the howling winds and dropping temperatures. Mary Gladys was walking outside to bring Scout, her seven-year-old Labrador retriever, an extra blanket when, wearing only a nightgown and a light coat, she slipped and injured herself; she lay immobile on the frozen ground.

Hearing his mistress's cry, Scout carried an old quilt from his doghouse to cover Mary Gladys, while Little Bit, an eleven-month-old Lab mix, squeezed through the glass storm door into the house and retrieved his mistress's glasses. Both dogs then lay down beside their mistress to keep her warm until help arrived the next morning.

—Michael Capuzzo

Sheila

It was a terrible night in the English mountains. The American B-17 crew became lost en route from their base in East Anglia to a raid on Germany. They thought they were flying at five thousand feet, but were at only two thousand. The farmers, in their kitchens, heard the crash.

It seemed a mission impossible—two men and a dog struggling through the night on a blizzard-swept mountain in December 1943, searching for a crashed bomber.

Shepherds John Dagg and Frank Moscrop were about to give up. But Mr. Dagg's sheepdog, Sheila, began darting back and forth, urging them to climb higher.

Trusting her instinct, they carried on—and found the wreckage of the American B-17 Flying Fortress. Two of the crew were dead, but four survivors were stumbling about in the snow.

The shepherds helped the fliers to the safety of Mr. Dagg's farm and, minutes later, the plane's bomb load exploded. Then Mr. Dagg's eighteen-year-old daughter Margaret cycled four miles to the nearest phone to raise the alarm.

Fifty-two years later, Margaret, now Mrs. Marshall, returned to the windswept peak of the Cheviots, near Kirknewton, Northumberland, to watch the Duke of Gloucester unveil a plaque commemorating the hero-ism.

"It was a terrible night," Mrs. Marshall recalled. "The plane came over low and then we heard it crash. My father set off with Sheila, and Frank joined him.

"There was a thick mist, and it was Sheila who found

the bomber. She sensed there was something there that shouldn't have been and led them straight to it.

"The airmen had been in our kitchen only about two minutes when the bomb load went off and shattered the windows. I cycled off to get help. We never felt we had done anything out of the ordinary—it had to be done."

"It was a mighty fine sight to see those two guys coming toward us with their dog," said one of the American airmen, seventy-year-old Mr. Berly, from South Carolina.

Sheila was awarded England's highest prize for animal valor in war, the Dickens Medal—the animal Victoria Cross—the only civilian dog to receive it. One of her puppies was later sent to the widow of one of the men who died in the crash.

—Roger Scott

One Miracle Deserves Another

A.C. was hours from being put to sleep when the Stafford family decided to adopt the Chesapeake Bay retriever from the pound.

Shortly after his own life was saved, the three-year-old dog showed his gratitude by pulling the Staffords' nineteen-month-old son out of a lake near their

Pontotoc home, and refusing to leave the tot until help arrived.

"It's unbelievable. It's a miracle," D'Anne Stafford said, "God used the dog to save our baby."

Stafford said she had been doing yard work while little Nolan toddled around. The boy apparently wandered about three hundred yards down a steep hill to a boat dock. She searched for her son, finally running down to the dock, where she found his hat at the end of the pier. Farther down the bank she spotted a soaking-wet Nolan, lying facedown on the ground, with A.C. at his side.

Doctors didn't know how long Nolan had been in the water, but told the family his core temperature had dropped to eighty-seven degrees. The boy has recovered fully, his mother said.

The Chesapeake is more powerful than other retrievers and is bred for waterfowl hunting. Their webbed feet and water-repellent coats make them superior swimmers. The breed's heart is the same as all other dogs'.

—Associated Press

The Shepherd Who Knew

Kate, an old shepherd bitch, lived in a house with a middle-aged couple and the wife's mother. The couple worked and came home late at night, barely saw the mother for supper, then rushed off to work the next morning.

But on weekends they began to notice Kate's strange behavior. Every time Grandma approached a wall or piece of furniture or went close to the basement door, Kate blocked her path. There was no doubt Kate was overstepping her bounds; and if she wasn't careful, she could very easily trip the old lady.

Then one Sunday, it all became clear. The husband asked for cauliflower, and Grandma passed him potatoes. The elderly woman was going blind—and only Kate knew. Kate had been protecting the woman for months when the couple didn't have a clue.

—Bill Tarrant

The Water Rescuer

In 1983 a powerful blizzard struck southern New Jersey. On Friday, February 11, blinding snow and gale-force winds buffeted the town where Andrea Anderson and her sisters, Heather and Diane, lived.

The three girls bundled up and went outside, but Heather and Diane soon went back indoors, leaving Andrea to play in the snow by herself.

The wind blew harder and colder, so Andrea decided that she too had had enough. As she started back to the house a powerful gust threw her forty feet down an embankment into a deep snowdrift.

Andrea began crying and calling for help, but because of the howling wind, no one could hear her.

No humans, at least.

In the house next door, Villa, a Newfoundland, approached the door and silently indicated to her master, Dick Veit, that she wanted to go out. Dick opened the door, and his dog lumbered out into the snow. When she heard Andrea's cries for help, the dog jumped a five-foot fence and made her way through the drifting snow to where the girl was trapped.

Villa immediately began licking the frozen tears off the girl's face, then methodically stamped down the surrounding snow. Finally Villa stopped still and thrust her head toward the girl. Andrea put her arms around Villa's neck and the dog pulled her out of the snowdrift. After an arduous trek—fifteen minutes to cover forty feet—Villa returned the girl to her doorstep, then made her way back to her own house and collapsed exhausted by the fireplace.

—Jon Winokur

King

It was Christmas Eve when Howard and Fern Carlson returned to their home in Granite Falls, Washington, and found a young, unwanted, injured, whimpering dog, who had been left on their grounds.

"Our old German shepherd had died just a few weeks earlier," said Mrs. Carlson, "and I was determined we weren't going to have another dog. The loss had been too great. But it was cold and the poor animal was hurt, so we decided to take him in for a few days."

King, a mutt, joined the Carlson household. "He and our daughter, Pearl, then ten years old, became insepa-rable," said Mrs. Carlson. "King has a wonderful tem-perament and loves children. Our grandson rides on him like a pony."

Last Christmas, disaster struck the household. The Carlsons were sleeping, and King was in the recreation room. A sliding glass door was left open a trifle, so he could go out when he desired.

Suddenly a fire flared in the utility room, which sepa-rated the recreation room from the rest of the house. King sensed the danger. Instead of running outside to safety, he fought his way into the fire, clawing and chewing through a plywood door that barred him from the blazing utility room.

Once through the door, the dog raced through the smoke and flames into Pearl's bedroom. She roused the family. "Howard was just back from the hospital, where he had been confined after an attack of emphysema," said Mrs. Carlson. "I called to Pearl that our best chance was to go out her window. I followed her out, thinking Howard was behind us. Then we heard bark-ing from inside the house. I climbed back and found

Howard had slipped and was on the floor, with King barking furiously beside him. The smoke now was very bad. I was able to get Howard up and King led us to the window, where we managed to escape."

King's paws and legs were badly burned, his mouth punctured with splinters and there was a long gash on his back that he suffered in getting through the plywood door. "King was the best Christmas present we ever received," said Mrs. Carlson.

—*Walter R. Fletcher*

Semper Fido

One night on Okinawa, army rangers and a demolition team attached to the 3rd and 4th Marine divisions were scouting in advance of the front line when the Japanese encircled them.

With no radio communications, and no escape, Robert Harr turned to his dog, Rex, a German shepherd trained by the Marine Corps to act as a scout and messenger. Sometimes, scout dogs like Rex could smell Japanese snipers or troops a full quarter-mile away, and would quietly brush up against their masters' legs to warn them.

Harr tied a note to Rex's collar, patted him, and ordered him to "find Robert," another handler back at camp. Rex raced off.

"He was shot in the front left leg," Harr said, "but he followed the trail back about four miles." Marine flares and support arrived to lead the trapped Marines back. Rex was credited with saving 150 lives.

From that day on, the men insisted on calling Rex by a new name—Oki. It stuck.

Oki accompanied Harr behind enemy lines on Saipan, Guam, Iwo Jima, and Okinawa. They were part of a high-explosives commando team that sneaked into Japanese cities ahead of American troops—blowing up safes to capture Japanese documents.

Oki took part in four South Pacific invasions alongside Harr. He was wounded in battle—shot and bayoneted.

But at war's end, the dog that saved hundreds of American GIs in action was scheduled to be killed— deemed too vicious for civilian life. Harr got the news while recovering from a knife wound in the Fleet Hospital in Guam.

"A minister came over to see me and said they were eliminating the war dogs," Harr said. "I said, 'By golly, I'm not going to let my dog go. He's been through everything with me.'"

The minister agreed to make the rounds of cargo ships in the harbor, looking for one that would carry the dog. Two days later, Harr and Oki boarded a Liberty ship en route to San Francisco.

From there, Harr shipped the dog back to his parents in New Jersey. He instructed his father to train his shotgun on the crate, and be prepared to kill the dog if it attacked anyone when freed.

A group of about fifteen neighborhood kids gathered around as Harr's mother coaxed the dog out, dangling a pair of her son's old moccasins in her hands. Oki dropped to his haunches and licked her hands.

"Just like that, he identified my mother with me," Harr said.

It took Harr nine months to retrain Oki. On weekends, he would muzzle the dog and walk him through New York's Chinatown to teach him that Asians no longer posed a threat.

President Harry Truman invited the dog to the White House, where Oki received the American War Dog Medal—the highest award for war dogs. That, with his Bronze Star, Presidential Citation, American Defense Medal, Asiatic-Pacific Campaign Medal, and Victory Medal, made him the third most decorated dog of the war.

When Oki died of cancer at age sixteen, he was given a full military funeral at a small animal cemetery in Costa Mesa. A Marine bugler played taps as a Marine honor guard saluted.

His tombstone was engraved, "Oki, A Marine Veteran, Semper Fidelis." That was 1958. Every Memorial Day for the next thirty-nine years, Robert Harr visited the grave site. "He was the smartest, most devoted friend I ever had," Harr, seventy-two, said during his last visit, holding a black-and-white picture of Oki. The old Marine sergeant softened, fought back tears and spoke haltingly.

"We honor the dead because they gave their last measure of devotion," Harr said. "And we honor those animals because they were devoted to helping these men survive. I usually bring flags. I usually salute him. And I usually bring along some flowers."

When Harr's wife, Diane, fell ill with multiple sclerosis, his frequent visits to Oki's grave dwindled. But in recent years, an anonymous Marine started caring for the grave. Each Memorial Day, talk would swirl about the Marine dog and the unknown mourner who visits the grave of the dog who gave his last measure of devotion.

—*Tom Berg, adapted from*
the **Orange County Register**

CHAPTER SEVEN

Reaching Your Dreams

Great men always have dogs.

—Ouida

Debra's Angel

When I first thought about getting a service dog, I thought of a beautiful golden retriever that did everything perfectly. But life doesn't always match our dreams, and that's not what I ended up with.

Instead, I got Emily, a two-year-old otter hound, who was rescued from a shelter by Freedom Service Dogs, Inc. in Lakewood, Colorado, on the day she was scheduled to be euthanized. She had been adopted and returned to the shelter three different times. Although she had a reputation for being stubborn, the Freedom Service Dogs staff were convinced that she was something special. After six months of training, she was matched with me.

Emily can do everything that I cannot do. I love to watch her run, because I can feel the freedom that she feels. Therefore, it's like I am running myself. When I hear the sound of her footsteps, it makes me feel strong, because I know she is not going to let me fall and hurt myself.

I have cerebral palsy. I used to fall all the time. My balance was so bad at one time that my doctor wanted me to start using a wheelchair. Now it is a big joke between us that Emily has proven him wrong.

Before I got Emily, I used to need help all of the time, but people on the street never took the time to care. I remember the winter before I got Emily when I had to go to work in a really bad snowstorm. I was too afraid to cross the street because it was very icy. So, I sat on the street corner for an hour in fifteen-degree weather trying to get up the courage to ask someone to help me cross the street.

Since Emily entered my life, there has been a big difference. Last winter I was walking the same route under the same conditions. Three different people asked if they could help me. It was nice to say, "Thank you, but now I can do it myself."

One of the biggest changes in my life is that I have had to readjust to people staring at me. They used to stare because I walk funny and talk funny, and I always hated it. But now, they stare out of amazement.

They wonder how I can handle such a big dog, and they see the love between us. One of the nicest things about having Emily is when I walk through the stores that I go to a lot, I hear people whisper about Emily and me. They say, "What a sweet dog she is."

Emily also makes things easier at home. I think every mother worries about their kids being ashamed of them, but in my case, it was a bigger worry than usual. Just before school started this year, my eleven-year-old daughter had two friends over to stay the night. I was so scared that she would be laughed at because of me.

Because of Emily, they could not have cared if I was purple with green spots. Emily gives me the time I need for people to see past my handicap and see the real Debbie.

I would like to share a poem with you that I wrote to my dad.

Daddy's Dream

Daddy wished his baby girl could walk.
Daddy wished his baby girl could talk.
My Daddy wished that I could run, laugh and play.
Daddy died before this dream came to be.

Daddy, do you see me laugh?
Daddy, do you see me run and jump and play?
Daddy, do you know that God has set me free?

—*Debra Angel*

The World's Most-Traveled Dog

Outside, a bitter wind whipped around the corners of buildings, and the windchill factor dipped to a frigid low. Albany, New York, was one of the coldest spots in the nation that winter night in 1888.

Shivering in the icy gusts of wind, a small dog roamed the dark streets of the town, seeking shelter. Everywhere doors were tightly closed against the wintry blasts. The dog, too cold even to notice the pains of hunger that gnawed at his stomach, came at last to the post office. Here he found an opening, a place he could be protected from the cold breath of Mother Nature.

Inside, a pile of empty mail sacks looked like heaven to him. He gratefully crept into their midst, sinking down into a pocket of softness. His tired bones eventually began to warm and he fell into exhausted sleep.

Next morning, postal clerks arriving to begin their day's work found him still there. No longer quite as cold, but much hungrier, the scrawny mutt aroused their sympathy. They couldn't find it in their hearts to send him back out into the streets to fend for himself. Instead, they shared their lunch with him and allowed him to stay in the post office.

Days passed and no owner showed up to claim the little stray. The postal workers had quickly grown fond of him. They cleaned him up and made an official place for him to sleep—in the corner of the office. And, so that he need no longer be an unknown wanderer in the cold, dark streets, they named him "Owney."

Little did they dream then of the adventures and fame their small, mousy-brown dog would have in the years to follow. For Owney was destined to become a world traveler, recognized and welcomed by postal workers everywhere.

Unlike the pony of the Pony Express and the eagle of today's U.S. Postal Service, Owney became a real live mascot of the United States mail.

After the first bitterly cold night when he found shelter in the Albany post office, Owney looked on mail bags as his special haven. Wherever he found a mail sack was home to him. He especially liked riding on top of the pouches when the mail was taken to the train depot in horse-drawn wagons.

One day he watched with bright-eyed interest as the pouches were transferred from the wagon to the train. The crew of postal workers called him aboard with them, and the friendly little dog accepted the invitation. He followed his beloved mail sacks onto the Railway Post Office mail car and made himself at home.

That first train ride with the U.S. mail took him to New York City. And this was only the beginning. Owney soon endeared himself to all the Railway Post Office crews, and they were glad to have him accompany them on their runs.

Trains were a principal mode of mail transportation in Owney's day, and he spent weeks at a time on the road, wandering farther and farther from his original postal home. He traveled to so many cities that the Albany post office workers were afraid he might get lost. They fitted him with a collar tagged with his name and address. On it, they asked that postal clerks in places he visited add tags to show that Owney had been there.

Owney collected those tags for almost ten years. He had them from all over the United States, from Alaska, from Canada, from Mexico. Finally there were so many that his collar could no longer hold them all. So the postmaster general ordered a special jacket for Owney to wear with all his tags attached. Owney wore it proudly as he set out on even greater adventures.

Just as he followed mail sacks aboard a train in Albany, so he followed them aboard a steamer bound for the Orient. He set out from Tacoma, Washington, and under the personal care of the ship's captain, arrived safely in Japan. There he was introduced to the emperor, who added a tag to Owney's jacket. His next stop was China, and on the homeward journey he collected medals in Hong Kong, Singapore, Algiers, and Port Said. Home again, he disembarked in New York City, hopped aboard a Railway Post Office mail car and headed back to Tacoma. Owney had traveled all the way around the world in 132 days—good reason for his reputation as "The World's Most-Traveled Dog."

Owney's life was filled with adventures. His travels abounded with escapades worthy of any hero of the roads. Once he was taken prisoner and held captive on a chain in a logging camp. The president of the railroad, determined to free him, stopped a train and dispatched a rescue unit. Owney was brought trium-

phantly "home" to the mail car, where he was, once
again, able to sleep on his cherished mail bags.

Another adventure put him on the wrong side of the
law in Canada. That time, his Albany friends took up a
collection in the office and bailed him out.

After nearly ten years of Owney's adventurous feats,
the post office department felt the time had come for
him to settle down. By then he had only one good eye
and could eat nothing but soft food. He deserved quiet,
relaxation and good care for the rest of his days. They
planned a retirement party in San Francisco. Owney,
used to public appearances at dog shows, had a fine
time at the celebration. He walked on stage, wearing
his jacket with its one thousand and seventeen medals,
before an audience of wildly cheering Railway Post Office clerks from all over the United States.

After the party Owney returned to Albany with his
special friends, the clerks who had found him that first
cold winter day. There he was supposed to stay and
enjoy his retirement.

But Owney had a strong streak of independence. He
also had a mind of his own. One of the tags he wore
bore this poem:

Only one Owney,
And this is he;
The dog is a loney,
So let him be.

It described him well. Owney had no intention of
being confined to one place when the whole world was
full of mysteries, adventures and mail bags. He slipped
away one day and set off on one final trail. He got as far
as Toledo, Ohio. There he died as he had lived, on the
road with postal friends around him. The little globe-

trotter would travel no more; his rambling days were done. Or were they?

Owney never followed his mail bags onto a plane, but his was a high-flying spirit. It isn't hard to imagine him still perched atop stacks of mail pouches winging their way to Zanzibar or Timbuktu. As long as mail carriers transport mail in sacks, the memory of Owney will follow them, medals jingling as he bounces along in search of new adventures.

—*Leila Dornak*

Benamino! Te Amo! *(Benji®! I Love You!)*

I grabbed Carolyn's hand as we stepped off the train. A nervous chill of anticipation skittered up my spine. People were rushing past us, anxious to get on with their morning, and we timidly tried to keep up. Someone spoke, and smiled, then spoke again, and hurried off. The words meant nothing, but we smiled back just the same.

It was our first trip abroad and my first time out of the country except for three days in Nassau and a few hours in Juárez. So maybe you can imagine. I mean, anywhere would've been terrific, but we weren't just anywhere. We were in Rome!

The Eternal City. Born nine hundred years before Christ. Home of Cato, Nero, Constantine, and the Caesars. A magical place where it is said you can actually hear the breathing of the centuries. And here it was, coming at me as a splash of bright sunlight at the end of a crowded train terminal.

Rome.

We emerged into the Piazza del Cinquecento and it took our breaths away. Mouths agape, we stood for a long moment, feeling every bit like hillbillies come to town. Then suddenly my heart stopped.

There before me, across the piazza, ten thousand miles from home, forty feet wide on a huge billboard, was my small, scruffy notion of a dog conceived in the shower one morning back in Texas.

Benamino!

Our first Benji movie was taking Rome by storm.

What an extraordinary feeling! The whole world seemed to grind to a stop. Everything froze in place for a moment as the realization sank in. We had been working incredibly hard, running, seemingly, at light speed for more than two years, raising money, writing script, shooting the picture, promoting, distributing. Always looking forward to the next problem, the next market, the next plateau; never really slowing down enough to look back at what had been accomplished. To fully realize, to absorb, to enjoy.

It was all against the tide, swimming upstream.

The experts, without exception, had said it couldn't be done.

It seemed like only moments ago that I was squinting through the dense smoke of a huge, black cigar at a balding, bug-eyed Hollywood salamander who was hissing, "It's a bad picture. Paramount has no interest."

Paramount wasn't alone. The first Benji movie was turned down by every major distributor in Hollywood.
Somewhere behind us a woman shrieked. Carolyn and I spun around. A wave of humanity was surging, racing, screeching frantically toward the terminal entrance. I was certain that some terrible disaster had befallen us, until, out of the melee, I heard the jubilant yelp of a small child. *"Benamino! Te amo!"*

Benji and his trainer were just emerging into the piazza. I turned to Carolyn, and she smiled. She must have known what I was feeling. Emotions were rushing through me like a river. I wanted to reach out and hug everybody in sight. Instead, I burst into tears. Carolyn slipped her arm around my waist and we turned back to the billboard and just stood there for a very long time.

Even today, I'm still in awe of Benji's success. I find it impossible to describe the feeling of being able to appear on a street corner virtually anywhere, say one word, and see eyes light up with so much love and affection.

To have been able to pass through this life and leave behind something that makes people feel so good keeps me forever aware that it has been a worthwhile trip.

Carolyn smiled, and I reached for her hand.

"Must be a star," Carolyn said.

"Overnight success," I whispered.

She smiled, and I reached for her hand. It was a warm autumn day. A light breeze was blowing. We were half a world away from home, standing in a beautiful Roman piazza, absorbing, seeing, realizing for the very first time the results of our labors . . . and it felt good.

I've spoken a lot over the past few years, especially to students, and have been heartened by the results. I've found that one of the most exciting, extraordinary things you can do with your life is to realize your dreams and help others do the same. It not only breeds happiness and a feeling of enrichment, it tends to make the world a better place. And why else are we here, but to leave things a little better than we found them?

The American dream, after all, is alive and well. The warranty that you can be whatever you want to be, no matter how impossible it may seem, if you want it bad enough to work hard to achieve it. That axiom I was taught early on, yet I'm still mystified that it's true. That it works. But it does.

The trick, of course, is that it's not always an easy road, or a short one. I thought I knew what I wanted to do with my life, become a filmmaker, when I was eight years old. I was certain I knew by the time I was sixteen. I was thirty-four before I was doing it.

Of course, there's always risk attached. The risk of losing. But it's a risk that must be taken in any serious effort to accomplish a difficult goal. You have to step out on the end of the diving board and leap off into the water. It simply doesn't work any other way. I suppose the thing that has always kept me out in front of my fears was the burning desire to see things done as well as they could be done. Being different never seemed very much like taking risks to me if I thought something was going to be better for the effort. But neither winning nor losing ever happens when you're sitting in the stands. You must be in the arena. Teddy Roosevelt said it better than I ever could. His credo has never failed to fuel the fires that continue to burn inside me, and I read these words often:

It is not the critic who counts, not the man who points out how the strong man stumbled or where the doer of deeds could have done better. The credit belongs to the man who is actually in the arena; whose face is marred by dust and sweat and blood; who strives valiantly; who errs and comes short again and again; who knows the great enthusiasms, the great devotions and spends himself in a worthy cause; who, at best, knows the triumph of high achievement and who, at worst, if he fails, at least fails while daring greatly, so that his place shall never be with those cold and timid souls who know neither victory nor defeat.

It was a fine fall morning in Paris, crisp and clear, and Benji was quite full of himself, cavorting near a fountain, playing with the children who had inexplicably materialized out of nowhere at the first whiff of a movie star. Their faces were radiant, and they took turns gently stroking his head. Those Benji chose to favor with a big sloppy lick exploded with laughter; and one young girl ran to her mother, screeching in French that she would never wash her face again.

A younger boy, perhaps eight, stood alone, apart from the crowd, a conspicuous shyness depriving him of the fun. I slid away from the camera, walked over and took the boy's hand and led him through a jungle of groping arms to what I imagine was his first kiss from an international superstar. He beamed up at me; and for that moment, in his eyes, I was king of France, maybe of the world. For this was no ordinary canine, this was the embodiment of all the emotions he had felt while snuggled in a dark corner of a theater somewhere in Paris, living Benji's desperate struggles as if they were his very own.

How well I understood. The smile I returned was

genuine, for this was the best reward of all. The very best.

—Joe Camp
Benji® is a registered trademark of Benji Associates;
excerpts from **Underdog, Longstreet Press.**

Angus's Ashes

I drifted through high school in a small town in the northwesternmost corner of New Jersey. My father had brought my mother and me there in 1939. He left us there in 1945 and never returned. We lost our big house on the edge of the woods and for the next fifteen years or so, we moved from one bad apartment to another.

My brother was born the year my father left, so my mother was stuck with me, my brother, and two big old dogs that belonged to me.

The woods were still within walking distance, so I spent as much time in them with the dogs as I could. Walking with my dogs in the woods, I felt longings I couldn't put into words. I felt strong and free. About this time I started to become interested in painting with watercolors, and the woods were the perfect subject.

When the dogs got too old for long walks I would go by myself to walk the woods and to paint.

When I look back I realize that my dogs were not only my best friends but were my early guardians on my journey. They were showing me the way to my destiny: to be an artist. And they were leading me to Angus.

High school was difficult. I was careless and carefree. A teacher in my Newton, New Jersey, high school once booted me from study hall, yelling, "Go take an art class!" In my senior year the school had an art show in a park in the center of the town. I sold all my watercolors and made fifteen dollars! I was hooked. I was going to be an artist even if it killed me.

After graduation I went to work in an A&P, caught pneumonia, and found a job at a local brassiere factory. I could draw, but had no idea how to apply my talent. My mother urged me to stay with my dependable factory job. At twenty, I felt my life had hit a dead end. I didn't feel much like making it to twenty-one.

In 1956, a local artist saw some of my paintings. His advice was blunt. "You'll always be a bum if you continue the way you're going," he said.

He was R. H. Buenz, a master craftsman and designer, and his words struck something inside. That year I began a four-year apprenticeship with him in the ancient and honorable craft of stained glass.

Four years later, in 1960, I left the North Jersey woods as a journeyman craftsman to spend the next four years in New York City to work at the craft and continue my studies as a fine arts student.

Four years turned into seven. I lived in the Village in a three-room cold-water apartment on the West Side. In 1965, at a party, I met an art student named Jonelle, the woman who became my wife. Our daughter, Tracy,

was born the next year in Greenwich Village. But that
winter I ran out of work in New York. I hated to leave
the Village but I had no work and no money and a wife
and baby to feed.

At the time one of the biggest studios in the country
was in Philadelphia, so I got a job there and moved my
wife and daughter to Philadelphia.

It took me eight years, but by 1974 I had saved
enough to make a down payment on a big old house
with a yard near a large wooded park, Fairmount Park.

I had wanted a dog since I left home in 1960 and now,
at last, seemed to be a good time to get a dog.

I found an ad in the newspaper for a six-week-old
Labrador retriever. He was black so we named him
Angus. He was a joy from the first night we got him.

My daughter, Tracy, was in school and Jonelle got a
job, so Angus and I were home all day. My career was
going well, and I was designing windows at home full
time.

Angus and I would start the day with an hour or so
run in the woods, then home to work. Angus would
sleep under my drawing board. I would stop at noon,
have lunch with Angus, and go back to work. Angus
would go back under the drawing board till around
4:30; then he would start to get restless, and I would
quit and go for our long walk, two miles or so.

On Fridays we would walk to the bank to cash my
check, then to the local bar. I would have a glass of beer
and Angus would wait by my feet, then we'd head home
with a stop at the ice cream store for Angus. (The
owner knew him and would give him a cupful of ice
cream.)

In 1976, I received a summons to an artist's dream: a
commission to do a window in the National Cathedral
in Washington, D.C., the monumental building of the

last American cathedral. It was a success and two more quickly followed.

But things weren't going well at home. We had another daughter in 1977, Vanessa; and after that the marriage began to fall apart, my mother died, and I got sick with lead poisoning. Angus was there through it all. No matter how bad it got, I could always watch him sleek and black running across a green field or rolling in the snow making dog angels. He was such a joy. With Angus at my side, I found the strength to quit my job and open my own studio.

The National Cathedral was being built according to traditions from the Middle Ages. In 1985, Richard T. Feller—who held the time-honored post of canon clerk of the works, who had overseen the building of the west end of the cathedral for thirty-five years—gave me a commission to do the Reformation Window. It was a grand commission for a three-lancet clerestory window in the center of the south transept.

With Angus resting beneath my drawing board every day, I labored on this grand commission for two years. It was then, as I drew and imagined, that Angus had trouble breathing. It got worse every day until the vet said he needed a throat operation. Angus was two weeks in the hospital recuperating, the first time I had been apart from him in twelve years.

When he came home he was better, but only for a short time. He got weaker and weaker. Our long woods runs of the past became block-long walks, then short walks, and finally rides in the car to the edge of the woods.

Angus was dying, and there was nothing I could do but stay with him. We slept together on the floor in front of the fireplace. I stopped working to tend Angus and his fire, and it seemed to give him strength.

My big cathedral window was done and ready to be installed. The window had to be set from a catwalk about ninety feet above the cathedral floor—the catwalk being the only place in the building that the security force and bomb-sniffing dogs won't go. The cathedral is often used by the president and other dignitaries, so the security guys get a little nervous about letting anyone up there.

A crew in Washington was hired to install the window, scaffolding was set in place, and we were given a security clearance. Everything was ready for me.

But I couldn't leave Angus.

I called the clerk of the works and told him I could not come until Angus got better.

They delayed the window installation two weeks.

That week my best friend stopped eating and could no longer walk. I carried him to the vet for the last time, and he died there in my arms. I closed his eyes with my own fingers.

The window was dedicated on October 30, 1988. It was the biggest celebration I ever had for one of my windows. My daughter and I signed it. It was a great day!

But no Angus to come home to.

With tears in my heart, I put Angus's ashes on a shelf in my studio.

The cathedral was completed in September 1990. The canon clerk of the works put the last stone in place on the top of the southwest tower. The cathedral was done but the windows were not.

In 1994, the clerk of the works asked me to return to the cathedral to do one last window—a small two-lancet window in the east end of the cathedral in the chaplain's office. The subject was to be the raising of

Lazarus, who was raised from the dead after three days by Jesus.

This was my fifth window at the cathedral, and in all likelihood my last.

It took about six months to fabricate, and I installed it with my daughter Tracy and Jed Bortline. Jed and his father had been working on the cathedral since Jed's dad got out of the navy after World War II.

The window looked okay, but not terribly inspiring.

The clerk of the works and the building committee felt the same way.

They did not approve it.

Once the committee started to criticize the window, everyone had something they wanted changed. Half the window would have to go.

It seemed my charmed life at the cathedral was over.

To get it past the committee I would have to remove it, tear it apart, change a lot of the glass, put it back together and reinstall it—mostly at my own cost. Tracy and I went back to Washington, and with Jed Bortline we pulled the window out of the cathedral. A black day indeed. We brought it home and stuck it in a dark corner of the shop. I could not bear to look at it for the entire winter. But as spring approached, with hope anew, I began to work in earnest to correct my last commission for the great cathedral.

We redrew the full-size working drawings completely over, made new patterns, cut new glass. We talked to the German glassblowers and had the most spectacular sheet of glass that I have seen in years made just for this window. The color was double gold pink for the Christ figure.

Tracy cut the glass, I painted it and then she glazed it (put in the lead). That night we finished it, and put it on the easel so we could see it first thing in the morning with the sun streaming through it.

It looked good!

One last task, a simple but crucial one. Waterproofing or puttying. There are many new and varied methods used to make stained glass, but since the ninth century puttying has been the same. You take a scrub brush, you make the putty and you scrub it under the lead. No fun.

In most cases I don't bother much with either making or applying the putty, but this time was different.

I got the linseed oil, whiting, and lampblack—the major ingredients—to mix myself.

And one more thing.

Angus's ashes were in a tin box on the shelf in my studio. I never buried them, for fear that some day I would sell the house and have to leave him. I wanted him in a safe place, where I could always go to see him.

With joy in my heart, I knew that I had found it!

The last thing that went into that window was a handful of my beloved Angus's ashes. On August 2, 1995, the window was accepted unanimously by the building committee. It was later installed in the National Cathedral. Word was the reverend's aunt was very pleased to look at the window.

I am proud that you can see my work today at the cathedral; and your children's children will be able to see it, and their children, too; and I hope they'll draw from it some of the love and joy I put into it. There is the Healing Arts Window, the Angels of Ministration, the Protestant Stream of Christianity, a window in memory of Joe Morris Blumberg Jr., who died, at age five, with his best friend, a dog, by his side.

And there is the small window that lights the chaplain's office—the Raising of Lazarus. The clerk of the works praised the "clear narrative quality of the window's design and [the] choice of color of the important German stained glass—especially the double gold pink."

The putty that seals the glass is the secret in my heart.

The office of the canon clerk of the works is now closed. The cathedral, after more than half a century of labor, is done. And Angus is in a safe place for the coming millennium. After that, I'm sure we will be together again.

I am sure God knows how much I miss him and She will bring us back together again.

—*Charles Z. Lawrence, Master Craftsman*

Susan and Joe

Susan, a nurse, is five feet tall and a hundred pounds. Joe, a Great Dane–German shepherd, is a head taller, one hundred five pounds. Theirs is a love story. When they met, at the dog pound in Seattle, he was four years old, unneutered, "barking at everything, the attention span of a flea," Susan Duncan recalled. "Typical testosterone poisoning." But she was charmed. The big goof put his paws up on her shoulders, looked down at her like a big brother, knocked her over. Susan was weak, couldn't get up. The multiple sclerosis was bad that day. So Joe picked her up. Practically carried her to the car. Joe and Susan, Susan and Joe. It was an animal-shelter match made in heaven.

Within minutes after their first meeting, they moved in together.

Joe works the ATM machine, does the laundry, opens the refrigerator door, fetches eggs. Susan said, "No, Joe. We don't need the milk! It's so heavy he has to bite the carton hard and we get a milk fountain!"

Susan Duncan, now thirty-eight, was afflicted at nineteen with MS, a disease that short-circuits the nervous system's signals to the brain. Its cure remains a mystery. Joe, now eight, was gifted at birth with that canine need to help and love human beings.

Susan can't get out of bed without Joe. "In the morning when I open my eyes Joe is there to take the covers off. Heat worsens the disease and it's good to cool off. Joe pulls off the comforter and pulls my feet out of bed, grabbing my toes, swinging me gently out of bed. He's got a soft mouth. He brings me my cane in his mouth and I stand and get my balance."

Leaving the house is impossible without Joe. "He normalizes my gait, keeps my balance. Before Joe, if I fell down, I'd have to wait for someone to find me. Now if I fall down, he lies next to me and pushes me up so I can assume an upright position. I'd be in a wheelchair without him."

In the city, Joe pushes open the doors of office buildings for Susan, helps her find her car when she forgets where she parked it, acts as a guide dog when her vision goes bad, locates bathrooms.

"What I find remarkable is he has never taken me to the men's room," Susan said.

"My fingers are so numb, I can't grip the money [at ATM machines], and it blows all over the parking lot.

One young boy took my money and ran. Joe gets the money out of the slot and the receipt and gets the card out of the slot for me. No one takes money away from Joe."

Susan, however, won't give her companion her PIN number. "He'd clean me out," she said, laughing, "buy out the dog biscuits, head for Mexico. He can open the front door, open the car door. It'd be the last I'd see of Joe."

—Susan Duncan and Michael Capuzzo

Barry

I once read a newspaper article about a German shepherd named Barry. He lived in Bonn, Germany. The landlord of the people who owned Barry didn't like dogs. He told the owners that they would either have to get rid of Barry, or move out. They didn't want to move out or to give up Barry.

But they had to make a decision, so they sold Barry to an Italian ice cream dealer named Angelini. And Mr. Angelini moved from Germany back to his hometown at the tip of the Italian boot, taking the dog, Barry, with him. Later, he reported to the family in Germany that the dog was missing, and he presumed the dog was dead.

One year later, having traveled twelve hundred miles on foot, walking from the tip of the Italian boot to Bonn, Germany, the dog scratched on his former owner's door—exhausted, unkempt, and footsore. He lay down at his master's feet, and pleaded with him, through those eyes of a dog, *I didn't want to leave you, and I have come back to you.* So the family and the dog moved into another house.

If a dog will walk twelve hundred miles for one year to obtain his objective, why won't a human being keep trying again, and again, and again? Perhaps he doesn't have sufficient *desire*. Now if, with all your heart, you truly seek, you shall find. People who truly try are people who accomplish things!

—*Norman Vincent Peale*

CHAPTER EIGHT

On Healing
and Faith

Snowflake

Every winter as the snow begins to fall, I rush outside to catch the first snowflakes as they silently fall toward winter's earth. This always brings back a childhood memory of being told that each snowflake is different and unique; and if we are lucky enough, someone or something that special will enter our lives. Little Annie was John's snowflake, and this is their story. . . .

It was particularly cold that February in 1989 as winter's frigid wind knocked hard at the large bedroom window. John was at home recuperating from surgery, and he and Annie were snuggled under a thick blue comforter. Her tiny body was pressed against his thin six-foot frame as her coal-black eyes darted toward the sound. Her muscles remained still as she let out a throaty growl, as if the snarl would scare the chill away. John could almost hear the brave four-pound Maltese say, "I'll protect you," as if she believed she were a hundred-pound German shepherd who could protect him from all the evil in the world. John had owned the two-year-old Maltese only for a year, but the two were closer than most people.

Annie had been a "throw-away" dog. Her previous owners had hopes that she would be a champion show dog and eventually give birth to champion puppies. However, she wasn't show-dog quality, and when she gave birth it almost killed her. The owners believed Annie wasn't good for anything, so they put an advertisement in the paper for a "free dog." The moment John saw the little ball of fluff, it was love at first sight. John saved Annie from certain death, and what John didn't know was that she was going to do the same for him.

John had always been healthy, but the stress from the job he loved as a police lieutenant and the emotional strain of a deteriorating marriage were more than his heart could take. On December 10, 1988, John suffered a massive heart attack, and the left side of his heart was destroyed. His mother and three brothers, who all live in Texas, were told to come quickly. John spent the next twelve days drifting between life and death, every breath expected to be his last. The doctors told his family that John's only hope was a heart transplant; but they shook their heads sympathetically, stating that organs were hard to come by, and it would take a miracle for John to get a new heart in time.

On December 22, just a few days before Christmas, John received that miracle.

In January, John was well enough to leave the hospital. While recovering at home, he and Annie lay side by side, her tiny heart beating next to his new one. It was a difficult time for John, and he worried about the uncertainties of his future and his life. However, he found a wonderful inner peace in Annie's constant companionship. He spent his days stroking her little white head and feeling her warmth, life, and love. It made him feel that he too was alive. When winter's fury was replaced with spring's calm, John was well enough to return to work. Annie must have sensed that John was okay and began to spend time outside. She would stretch her tiny limbs and bask on the sun-warmed wooden deck in the backyard. Annie also liked to sneak up and bark at other dogs as they strolled by *her* fence. She almost seemed to laugh out loud when they appeared startled. She would then turn her head toward John, making sure he knew that she was protecting their domain. John would roar with laughter at the little ball of fluff's antics. John believes it was Annie's constant love that helped him regain his physical and mental strength during those emotionally critical months.

As summer crept into fall and fall's rich colors began to die, so did John's marriage. John cared deeply for his wife, but all the love in the world couldn't keep her from walking out the door a few days after Valentine's Day in 1990. Again, John had to start the recovery process, but this time it was from a broken heart. At night, John and Annie would lie in bed, and he would listen as she let out her throaty growl at winter's biting wind. John believed that Annie knew he was sad, and through the storms he could almost hear her say, "Don't worry, I'll always protect you."

For the next three years Annie saw John through broken promises and broken hearts. Then in the fall of 1993, just when John began to believe he was destined to spend the rest of his life alone, we met. Soon his broken heart healed, and we were married in June 1994.

Sadly, less than two months after we exchanged our wedding vows, little Annie dislocated her hip and suffered a fatal stroke. She died in John's arms. I had never seen John cry before, and I knew that his new heart was breaking. John was devastated. However, through his tear-stained blue eyes he stated he believed Annie's purpose in life was to watch over him while he healed, both physically and emotionally. And with that task fulfilled, it was time for her to watch over someone else.

Annie still watches over John as her small picture rests atop the fireplace mantel near the backyard window facing her beloved deck. That was almost three years ago. John and I now share our hearts, and queen-size bed, with two Maltese named Kitten and Max that were also throw-away dogs. However, each winter when the frigid wind howls against our bedroom window, John says he can almost hear his little snowflake whisper, "I'll always protect you."

—*C. Kay Bassett*

The Ultimate Protector

Jim Murray is a tall, rugged man with pale, piercing blue eyes, the receding hairline of a man in his forties, and a deep protective instinct. Jim has a lot of competition in the termite-control business in southern New Jersey, but there's only one ad in the yellow pages that says, "The Ultimate Protector." Jim Murray's. A few of his competitors snickered when Jim published his new ad, showing a cartoonlike superhero with a flowing cape and arms akimbo, like a larger version of Superman. But Jim stuck with it. He takes his job seriously.

Jim married once, and it didn't work out. He's got custody of his two children, whom he's very devoted to. But during some lonely years, his best friend was a dog, Bernie.

Jim discovered Bernie when he was treating for termites in a backyard in Pitman, his hometown. There in the yard was a huge, beautiful black-and-brown creature the size of a small horse with a giant black head and big orange Cravola-colored markings hooding the gentlest brown eyes Jim Murray had ever seen. He appeared to be a mix of a Newfoundland, a German shepherd, and some crazy, divine inspiration.

Jim wanted to know what the big dog was doing confined to a small cage. Jim reached out to pat his nose through the cage and the dog whimpered and gratefully licked his hand. "My husband and I are allergic to dogs," the woman of the house told him. "So we had to lock Brownie up. We're afraid to pet him."

The last thing Jim needed was a dog in his life, he figured. But he couldn't stand to see the dog cooped up like that. He planted his hands on his hips and said, "With all due respect, ma'am, I think you ought to give this dog over to me. I'll take good care of it."

The woman said okay, and by the time Brownie got home, riding shotgun in the termite-control truck, his name was Bernie.

Now Jim lives out in the country near Pitman, in a small house with some land, and he let his dog run. "Bernie was so smart," Jim said. "I'd just step out back and call for him once, and no matter how far away he'd come thundering right to my side. Oh, he was just the greatest dog you've ever seen."

There's not much traffic in Jim's area, but he did discourage Bernie's roaming, trained him to stay on the property. But one day Bernie, while crossing a quiet country road in front of the house, was hit by a speeding pickup truck. Jim had just stepped out of his house when he heard the sickening thud and saw his dog fly some twenty feet into the air. As the truck sped away, Murray ran across the street to tend to Bernie. As he got closer, he realized the impact was so great that an ordinary dog would have been instantly killed. Bernie, a muscular 120 pounds, crumbled to the ground and was wailing in pain. But as Jim approached, he was astonished to see his dog pull himself to his feet and hobble terribly, on three legs, under Jim's deck.

Bernie's front right leg was severed just below the elbow, hanging by a thread of skin. The dog growled and bared his teeth at his master, seeming to say, "Leave me alone to die." But Jim crawled under the deck and carried Bernie to his truck. The veterinarian in Pitman was unequivocal. "Jim, I'm sorry but there's nothing that can be done. He's so big, it's like a leg injury on a horse. We have to put him to sleep."

Jim refused to believe it. Tears in his eyes, his back straining under the load of his 120-pound dog, he carried Bernie back to the truck and drove to another veterinarian he knew in the next town. Getting the same response, he went to the yellow pages, dialed up another veterinarian. And another one.

Finally, a receptionist at an animal hospital told him to try across the river at the University of Pennsylvania in Philadelphia. Penn's veterinary hospital is one of the finest in the country. Murray drove his termite-control truck, carrying Bernie, there immediately. The specialist who could have helped him was on vacation in California but he was flying home that night.

The veterinary surgeon said that it was possible to save Bernie, but it was a long shot. And, furthermore, it would take an extraordinary commitment on Murray's part to make the surgery a success, a commitment that might very well be impossible. For three months, while the dog's leg healed, Murray would somehow have to keep Bernie totally immobilized. If the dog stood up just once on the injured leg, he would have to be put to sleep. If Jim could promise to do everything in his power to help his dog in the recovery period, the vet said he would perform the surgery. Jim made his promise.

The surgery was a success. Jim brought Bernie home in his truck. Then he carried his best friend out to the backyard, under a large maple tree close to the house, laid him down on his side, and staked him to the ground. Bernie could raise his head, but that was it. The dog whimpered softly, his brown eyes meeting Murray's, just as he had when Murray had rescued him from the cage. There was trust there now in the dog's eyes, complete faith.

Jim slept many nights alongside Bernie. It was summer, and they were blessed with good weather and little rain. The spot he had chosen under the tree was cool and shady. Jim fed Bernie by hand and kept him watered when the big dog panted in the heat. He cleaned up Bernie's messes with water, kept the grass and the earth around him clean. He petted and massaged him and spoke to him softly, telling him he would get better. Twice a day, he checked the wooden stakes and tightened them to keep them secure.

At last, in the autumn, when the maple tree had turned red and started to drop its leaves around Bernie, the day came when Jim loosened the stakes and Bernie stood, wobbly at first, on a fully healed leg. Murray took a day off from work to be with his dog, to celebrate as they romped together in the fields. "That dog is like my brother," he said. "I just couldn't let him go."

—*Michael Capuzzo and Jim Murray*

Vigil of the Cemetery Dog

My seventeen-year-old son was killed in a diving accident. Only a parent who has lost a child can understand the personal devastation. The evening before the accident, I happened to drive by our local cemetery. Sitting next to the fence was a stray dog. She sat on a small knoll between two trees, seemingly waiting for someone. She looked like a bedraggled red fox. Little did I know that three days later I would be burying my son on the exact spot where the little dog waited.

On the day of my son's funeral service, I saw the little dog again. She was standing a short distance away from where we gathered at the cemetery. The next morning, just before dawn, I went to visit my son's grave for the first time. And sitting beside the mound of flowers at his graveside was the little red dog. As I approached, she rose and stepped back a few feet, as if in respect. When I sat on the ground by the grave, she came back and sat beside me, not touching me or asking for attention for herself. She seemed to just be there for me. Together, we watched the sun rise, and I felt a slight touch of peace. I arose, and she walked me back to my car, then returned to my son's grave and lay down on it. The next morning was a repeat of the first. There she was, nestled beside the flowers. As she sat beside me, I ran my hand down along her back. She was slightly wet, as if from night dew. "You been here all night?" I asked. She answered with a slight wag of her tail. "What are you? Some kind of guardian angel?" She turned toward me and looked at me with eyes that seemed to reach my very soul. I began to cry and tell her of my terrible pain, and she sat and listened.

The next morning, there she was. Beginning to think

of someone besides myself, I had brought a bowl of food and some water for her. Apparently, someone else had noticed that the little dog was doing twenty-four-hour duty, because there was already a bowl of water by the grave. Knowing that my son wasn't alone, that he had this small dog with him, began to give me comfort. I remembered that several years before, my son and a friend had rescued a small red dog that had been shot with an arrow. My son named her Callie, and she stayed on as a beloved pet until an untimely accident took her life.

After about a week, I took the cemetery dog home with me. Strangely enough, she was quiet and subdued. I couldn't think of a name for her. Then one day, I said, "You know something? You look just like old Callie." It was as if I'd hit a magic switch. Callie stood up and, tail wagging furiously, ran over to me and put her paw up on my knee. It was as if she had finally come home.

Who is this dog who showed me my son's cemetery plot, and then did round-the-clock sentry duty when my son was laid to rest there? Who is this dog who was there to help me through the greatest trauma of my life, who now shares my home and helps fill the lonely moments? Is there such a thing as reincarnation, and are dogs reincarnated? I don't know. I just know that she came into my life in a very mysterious way. My other dogs couldn't give me the comfort that this little red dog did, and still does.

Callie has since become Therapy Dogs International (TDI) certified. I take her on regular visits to our local nursing home where she has become the adopted dog. I am very proud of Callie. During the days following the Oklahoma bombing, TDI-certified dogs—including my Callie—were taken to the rescue center and to the church where the victims' families were waiting. Callie, with her gentle way, made many friends. In an especially touching moment, a medical worker sat on the floor with her arms around Callie, petting her and sharing her personal pain. It reminded me of myself as I sat with Callie at my son's grave only the previous June. I'd never thought one way or another about angels or guardians but now I know there is such a thing.

—Doris Mitchell

Steven and Bumper

After suffering many illnesses since infancy, Steven Hensley was hospitalized the winter of his seventh year for seventy-eight days, undergoing four surgical procedures for the diagnosis and treatment of Hirschsprung's disease, a disease of the large intestine and colon.

He had arrived at the hospital suffering from high temperatures and the inability to eat. He weighed only forty-four pounds. His life was in jeopardy on more than one occasion.

"He was in a whole lot of pain," said his mother, Dawna Hensley. "Steven is not one to complain because he's known pain all of his life. But when it got too severe, he got scared, and that made it worse."

And then along came friendly Bumper, a black Labrador mix, and her owner Ken McCort, an animal behavior consultant and one of the first volunteer members of the Akron Children's Hospital Medical Center's Doggie Brigade.

"Bumper and Steven seemed to take a special interest in each other. When Bumper walked into the room, Bumper and Steven seemed to bring each other to life. When he was petting Bumper or when he had Bumper in bed with him [on a separate sheet], he would say, 'I love you, Bumper.' Bumper knew where and when to be gentle. She was the only one who could touch Steven's belly and could put her head there very lightly while Steven petted her or played with her ears."

On other occasions, Bumper helped her young friend socially with other children on the unit. Steven always had several tubes to deal with when he would go for a walk in the halls or to the playroom. He had one tube in his rectum and sometimes as many as five or six IVs going into his chest cavity. When moving about, he had to be extremely careful of these tubes, and had to be escorted by a staff member. His mother said this put a great deal of pressure on Steven, and as a result, he would go to the playroom only with Bumper beside him. The dog would act as a medium for interaction between Steven and the other children, putting everyone more at ease and making things seem more normal.

After one of his more painful surgeries, Steven was told he had to get up and walk around, something he was afraid to do because he thought his belly would hurt. His mother recalled that he was "walking like an old man in pain."

McCort, who had been visiting children on another floor of the hospital, heard that Steven was having a hard time and took Bumper to assist. He remembers seeing Steven bent over and fighting the several staff members that surrounded him. McCort called out, "Stevie! Bumper's here!"

Steven straightened up and greeted his canine friend with enthusiasm. When asked if he would like to take Bumper for a walk, he immediately agreed and walked off happily, up·and down the hallways.

"It was as if all his pain diminished," remembered Dawna. "He was like a new Steven, calling back to me, 'I'm walking Bumper, Mom!' "

McCort said that Steven grew so fond of the dog that he worried about the child when it was time to go home and they would be separated. Happily, Bumper got an autographed "see-you-later" drawing from Steven. Mc-Cort said the pair have seen each other twice since Steven's release, and Steven's mom said she'll soon be taking Steven to visit Bumper at McCort's farm in Doylestown, Ohio.

"A dog doesn't care if you're sick or well," she said. "They love you no matter what."

—Marla Kale

General Winfield

My grandmother resides at Surrey Place, a "progressive" nursing home in Chesterfield, Missouri. In 1992, two years after the home opened, a security guard who worked there was passing through Winfield, Illinois, and observed an eight-week-old puppy being "dumped" at a garbage site. The kind guard scooped the pup up and took it to work with him. He approached the director, Kim Olden, with the idea of keeping the pup there, and she answered, "Why not?"

With this, General Winfield, as he is now known, became a permanent resident of Surrey Place.

As a professional grief counselor and "dog person," I had my concerns. This was, after all, a shepherd-mix pup already fifteen pounds or so; what about temperament? Or worse yet, what if he jumped on the residents and knocked them down?

Much to my surprise and delight, this pup seemed to know exactly why he was there. While he would wrestle with visiting children, he never so much as "gummed" an adult. (The skin of elderly people is very fragile; he sensed even at his age not to "play bite.") He ran down corridors as most puppies would, but had an uncanny knack for knowing when a wheelchair or walker would pop out of a room.

Winfield's ability surpasses that of any grief counselor I know—and after fifteen years in grief counseling that covers a lot! All of the expertise I've ever learned, Winfield was born with, I realized, watching him work one incredible day.

One of the residents had an inoperable brain tumor. Her husband, a doctor, knew that death was imminent and wanted to be called when the time was near. He was phoned before his wife's death, but was unable to get there in time. This man had never been close to the staff or shared his feelings with anyone at the home. Despite many attempts to console him, he rejected all forms of help. In the past, he had never really acknowledged Winfield either, but when he went into his wife's room to be alone with her lifeless form, Kim noticed Winfield following him. She passed the door several times and saw the man sobbing as he hugged the dog. Winfield stoically sat there taking in the grief, supporting the griever, and simply doing his job. Although no written acknowledgment was received from the two-legged professional, to this day Winfield receives a box of dog biscuits every Christmas from this man.

—*Bonnie Rowley*

The Golden Moment

You might say our eyes—the dog's and mine—met across a crowded parking field one hot July day in 1988.

Widowed in October 1987, I had been comforted by our golden retriever, Josh, only to lose him six months later when he succumbed unexpectedly during an operation.

This particular day, I was on my way to a pool, when I made a quick stop to purchase a birthday card. As I approached the store, I noticed a woman and two young girls tying up what appeared to be a young golden retriever. There was that familiar gentle look in his eyes. I thought I might tactfully discourage the woman from mistreating the dog by tying him up outside and struck up a conversation explaining my partiality to golden retrievers and how mine had died recently. I learned he was a mixed breed, and then the woman made a startling comment, saying, "Would you like him?" She went on to list his attributes—that he was a neutered male, he would never get any bigger, he was clean and obedient, and he even had a doghouse. She explained that she and her husband both worked, and it was difficult giving the dog the care he needed, especially since he was very affectionate. I found myself considering her offer and asked the girls, "What do you think?" They were in agreement. The woman was saying, "I could bathe him and bring him to your house." Impulsively, I said, "No, I'll take him now!" The best decision I've ever made!

His name was Rocky, much to the delight of my young grandson. However, it just didn't suit this gentle dog, so I renamed him Buddy. And that is just what he has been, going with me everywhere. His favorite place was the nursing home, where he visited my mom and lifted the spirits of the other residents as well. Mom, known to everyone as Nana, died on her ninety-third birthday, May 15 of this year. In her last month, she extracted a promise from me to continue bringing Buddy to visit after she was no longer here.

On a lighter note, the day after I got Buddy, an open

truck came rumbling down my street carrying a neatly
shingled doghouse.

—*Elaine M. Shafonda*

The Life Retrievers

My great-grandfather was the gun-fighting sheriff of
Sedgwick County, Kansas, from the mid-1880s until
the turn of the century. When my father was a boy and
asked his grandfather why there were notches in his
gun, George Harvey made a comment recorded in the
"Harvey Family History": "I had to keep track of some
'critters' that I had to kill when I was sheriff." My
grandfather was Homer Wanda Harvey. George named
him after the Indian chief Wanda, from the Indian Na-
tions just one county away, who was a good friend of
his. With this type of heritage, my father, Red Harvey,
and his brother, Ron, wanted to be cowboys, despite
the fact that they were raised in Appleton, one of the
largest cities in Wisconsin.

My mother was raised in town, too. But she never
wanted to leave it. She hated animals. She wanted a
house with a white picket fence and security. She had
been raised in a large German Catholic family during
the Great Depression. She was a beautiful prima donna

who loved to be the center of attention in a crowd. Her father was brutally abusive, and her mother was neglectful.

Two people were never more mismatched than my mother and my father. Red was like Paul Maclean in *A River Runs Through It*. He was wild, handsome, and devastatingly charming. He had a bizarre sense of humor. On the other hand, my mother was deadly serious. She was totally self-centered, vindictive, and cruel.

My father fancied himself a rugged Ernest Hemingway type, so when I was a baby, he moved our family, the dog, and his fledgling mink ranch to the Upper Peninsula of Michigan. He bought a five-acre farm surrounded by miles of dense forest; our farm was merely a clearing in it. The nearest town was a wide spot on highway 2 called Gulliver, and it was five miles away. Hunters had become lost in the hundreds of miles of continuous forest.

There we had a two-story house, a barn, and a chicken house. The gravel road passed by the front yard. The barn was about two hundred feet behind the house, and the chicken coop was to the side between the house and the barn. There was a small creek with rainbow trout in it a quarter of a mile down the road.

My father worked for the local power company. To supplement his income and as a hobby, he raised mink. We had five horses.

I was my mother's first child. My mother was violently abusive, as a result of her brutal upbringing. When I learned to talk, some of my first words were, *shut up* and *sit still or I'll beat the* ——— *out of you.* My father did not know that she abused me.

When I was a toddler, she would lock me out of the house, as if I were a cat, so that she could go back to bed and sleep all day, because she suffered from migraine headaches and insomnia. She hated animals, but she did admit that our black Labrador retriever, the Duchess of Winchester, was "so smart that she was almost human." In spite of my mother's behavior, which is now considered to be felony child endangerment, she always made certain that Duchess was with me. My mother used Duchess as a baby-sitter.

Duchess never left my side. When I crawled and later toddled out into the road, Duchess would drag me by the suspenders back into the front yard. Later when I was between the ages of two and three and walked fast and spoke, I would give Duchess commands that she would obey and only she could understand. I would scream incoherently and point at our Rhode Island Red laying hens, and she would retrieve one for me to hold and pet.

One of my favorite things to do was to sit next to Duchess as she was standing beside me. I would bend from the waist and bounce my back repeatedly against her ribs, all the while humming to myself. This is a trauma symptom in abused children. By the age of two, I already had posttraumatic stress disorder from all of the physical and verbal abuse. I would crawl under the pasture fence and then under the bellies of the wild range horses to try to bounce against them as I did with Duchess. They would peer down at me between all four of their legs and carefully step around me.

When I walked all of the time instead of crawling as well (my mother said that I ran everywhere), Duchess began to follow me off the property to keep me from getting lost in the forest. Being a hunting dog, Duchess could always find her way home. At that point raiding the henhouse, eating dirt-covered onions and carrots directly from the garden, sharing table scraps thrown into the chicken coop, wandering into the pasture with the horses, pushing my baby sister into the well, and sticking my finger into a mink cage to be badly mauled were no longer entertaining enough for me. I had to explore. So I started to routinely walk the quarter of a mile down the road to the creek with its rainbow trout flashing in the sun-dappled water.

One day when Duchess and I arrived, we met a mother black bear and her twin cubs. The sow bear reared onto her hind legs and roared at us. As she began to charge, Duchess attacked her ferociously. Duchess's unexpected assault succeeded in aborting the bear's charge to protect her cubs. She whirled and ran into the dense forest with her cubs following closely behind.

My father bought Duchess to breed when there were only three thousand Labrador retrievers in the world. He bred Labs all of his life. Duchess was his first. He tried feverishly to breed her to male Labs with champion bloodlines like her own. She would have none of them at first. When she finally did, she only had one puppy, which died. Her main source of l'amour was mongrels, much to my father's disgust. After she succeeded in getting bred to a large shaggy mutt, she had ten puppies.

Duchess treated me like one of her puppies. I was included in the litter. When the pups started bounding around, they would hide from me behind a rocking chair in the corner of the living room because I played too roughly with them. Then, as they got older and bigger, they started to drag me around by the suspenders. That was when *they* played too roughly with *me*. So I began to hide behind the rocking chair from those rough-and-tumble pups. One day I found the head ripped off my favorite doll. I snatched the doll's body from the floor, and in rage I shouted at the pups, "Who did it? WHO DID IT?" I look back now and realize I fully expected them to understand, and perhaps they did. They were like brothers and sisters to me. They were my world.

At first the pups had smooth coats. They were all solid black and looked like purebred Labrador retrievers. As they got older, their coats got longer and wavier. My father would leave all of them together in the front yard from the time that they were eight weeks old. One by one all ten of them were stolen by passersby.

Unfortunately for me, this was the happiest time of my childhood. My mother left my father to marry one of his temporary employees. My mother's second husband was an alcoholic brute with shellshock who had been wounded in the back of the head in World War II. He was extremely violent. He hated me because I would not accept him as my new father. I hated him back. I was beaten with boards, sections of garden hose, and broom handles at least four times a week. He was so abusive that I regarded my mother as a source of comfort and protection from him. He killed almost every animal we ever owned. He shot our only dog to death with his shotgun. He butchered and forced my sister and me to eat our Easter bunnies. The cats that didn't run away from his abuse died.

There was no love for me in that household in Appleton, Wisconsin, and later Neenah. After I no longer saw my father, who moved to Kalispell, Montana, no one loved me except my father's parents. But I saw them only several times a year. The only source of unconditional love in my childhood was the love of animals. Without knowing why, I walked up to and befriended every dog that I ever saw. I was never bitten. I drew horses when I first began to use crayons. Naturally, I was never allowed to have a horse or a dog of my own. All I knew was that I loved all animals and that they were my special friends. Dogs and I always understood each other on even a nonverbal level.

When I was in my twenties and single, I bought a black Labrador retriever from my uncle Ron. She was bred from my father's dogs. In my thirties, I got my first horse, a Morgan mare. I bought a horse farm with my late first husband just outside of Raleigh, North Carolina. I did not understand until my father died and I went into trauma treatment for all of the child abuse that I had suffered that the only source of love in my daily life after my father was gone was that of animals. As a toddler I had bonded with all animals, but I had bonded most strongly with dogs. I am forty-nine years old. I have a master's degree, and I spent six years working on a doctorate in chemistry. But I found that I could not work because being around people was so stressful for me. Also, my physical health failed, and I became allergic to most chemicals.

I have severe posttraumatic stress disorder for which there is no cure. When I entered trauma treatment, I was congratulated for being alive. When I asked why, I was told that most people like me commit suicide, die in accidents caused by risk taking, die from drug overdoses, die at the hands of spouses and boyfriends, die as children in an abusive home, or die from cirrhosis of the liver or other diseases. A doctor said that they rarely lived to be my age. When I was suicidally depressed after my husband died, my Lab and even one of my horses used to hover over me, lick me, snatch the hat off my head and cavort around me to change my mood. The Arabian horse would act as if I were a cow, and he was a cow pony "cutting" me. He blocked my every move until I put both arms around his neck and hugged him. Then he would lick the tears from my cheek and be satisfied. The Lab, Gypsy, would lie at my feet, put her head on my lap and whine when I was the most down. She would get me to focus away from my agonizing grief.

During that terrible time when my first husband died, and I was left alone with my animals and could barely care for them because I was crushed by grief, my father's mother, Emeline B. Harvey, wrote to me from Wisconsin.

I got your letter yesterday. . . .

I'm sorry to hear you are so down. But remember you only have to face one hour, one day at a time. Do what needs doing such as taking care of your good horses. Gaily is too valuable to neglect her feet. Standing in muck will make her foot problems worse. And a horse without good hooves is worthless. So take good care of her. She'll appreciate it. And working with your pets (the dogs) will calm you too. Love is always reflected in love.

I'm glad you went to that widow's group sponsored by the Lutheran Church. You may be able to help one another a great deal. I know from my own experience that turning to God is a very present help in time of trouble. I've never been one to air my troubles much. So lifting my eyes above my problems and seeking Him has always helped. You probably won't believe this now but it works. It is our salvation. . . .

My dear, I wish I could take your troubles away.

Promise yourself you will not be defeated by this tragedy. Look to the Lord and He will uphold you. Now I hope and pray you will sort things out and life will begin to look brighter for you.

My love and God's blessings,
Grandma

I am now happily remarried to a man who loves animals as much as I do. He even strongly resembles my father physically. Animals continue to be my irreplaceable teachers and healers. I do not have children because child abuse has existed in my mother's family for at least one hundred and ten years.

We have three show horses and two dogs. I show in regional Arabian and Morgan breed shows each year and sometimes compete in the Grand National.

I would not be alive today to enjoy happiness, love, and financial success without the love and care of two black Labrador retrievers, the Duchess of Winchester and the Ebony Gypsy of Hortonia.

Growing up in a world where hate breeds more hate, they taught me that love begets love.

Everyone in this world needs someone to love them, and they were the first to love me.

—*Lynn Marie Harvey*

Boy

The dog family is a group of thirty-eight species of carnivorous mammals that includes the wolf, coyote, jackal, and domestic dog. Members of the dog family, like other carnivores, evolved from a genetlike, tree-climbing carnivorous mammal. Although once grouped with bears and raccoons, they are now considered to be more closely linked to cats in evolution.

The Lhasa apso was first recognized by the American Kennel Club in 1935. All colors are acceptable. The coat is heavy, straight, of good length, and very dense. Good whiskers and beard; black nose; and heavy hair on the face, forelegs, hind legs, and feet are breed requirements. The tail and body carriage must be very erect, regal in nature.

A glimpse at the definition of a dog and a Lhasa at this particular time in my life shows that by no means does a denotative definition describe what is in your heart. I'm writing this hoping it will be a type of therapy for me, as I have been told that when one is greatly distressed, writing about the situation may help to some degree. For you see, my Boy left this earth on Tuesday, July 23, 1996.

As I pulled into my driveway, the garage door was open, which is not normal. My husband had arrived home before me, which was unusual for him. He usually was not in town during the week, let alone arriving home early in the afternoon. My husband ran out the door, looking greatly distressed, as I exited the car. My first thought was that Susie, my youngest terrier, had gotten out, and we needed to start out after her. My other thought was that due to the storm of the afternoon Lady, my other terrier, had gotten sick, as she is gravely afraid of storms. My husband grabbed my shoulders as if to keep me from entering the house. I said, "What is the matter?"

He simply stated, "Boy is dead!"

"No, no," I screamed, "he was fine this morning. He ate his breakfast and was barking for more food when I left."

How do I define my Boy? My love, my life, my child, my son? I do not know. Most people are not dog people, so having as close a relationship with a dog as I had with Boy is hard to define.

I have no children. Boy was the closest to a child that I will ever have. Boy was my father's dog. My dad had a stroke when Boy was a year old, and I have had him since. My dad passed away in 1989, making me promise to always take care of Boy.

Boy died at fourteen years and eight months old. Boy was diagnosed with Cushing's disease, a liver disease, when he was approximately seven years old; and in May 1995, he was diagnosed with diabetes. He was on a special diet and medication and had two insulin shots each day.

Why did I keep Boy going? Partially, I guess, I was selfish; but true to his breed, Boy made the decision to go on. Time after time, he would bounce back as if nothing were wrong with him. He was a feisty little dog, barking for his food, master of the dog household in pecking order. He always demanded and received his way with me and the other dogs.

My veterinarian performed a postmortem and assured me that Boy did not suffer, that his heart just finally stopped. We buried him on Wednesday in a pet cemetery. I know that he will never be sick or suffer again, although I will suffer for some time to come.

Unfortunately, no one on this earth understands my

feelings for Boy. The people whom I work with think
that I am stupid for caring so much for a dog, spending
the time and money that I have over the years. My
husband cares about Boy, but even he cannot understand why I am so upset.

In closing, here is a poem I found that has helped. I
consider it Boy's testimonial to me. The author is unknown.

Don't grieve too long for now I'm free
I'm following the path God set for me
I ran to Him when I heard His call
I wagged my tail and left it all.

I could not stay another day
To bark, to love, to romp or play.
Games left unplayed must stay that way
I found such peace it made my day.

My parting has left you with a void
So fill it with your remembered joy
A friendship shared, your laugh, a kiss
Oh, yes, these things I too shall miss.

Be not burdened with times of sorrow
I wish you the sunshine of tomorrow
My life's been full, you've given so much
Your time, your love and gentle touch.

Perhaps my time seemed all too brief
Don't lengthen it now with undue grief
Lift up your heart and share with me
God wanted me now, He set me free.

—Lou Olinger

The Rainbow Bridge

I am a volunteer at the North Carolina State University Veterinary School in Raleigh, North Carolina. Our organization is called Friends Helping Friends. All pets seen at the school have been referred by their local veterinarian, so their problems are fairly serious. I work in the waiting room, where I greet and talk to the four-legged patients and their two-legged mommies and daddies who bring them in. We try to make both the four-legged and two-legged kind feel at ease.

I have a twelve-year-old Labrador, Shadow, and beginning with the start of the new television season last year, she became a critic. After a few minutes of listening to TV, she gets up and goes into the bedroom. She may have more sense than my wife and I do.

I have always loved animals, and I understand the tremendous feelings people share with me every day. It makes me feel better, knowing I'm helping people through their feelings of loss, which are universal. Someday I know someone will help me when I need it.

In addition to the waiting room in our clinic, we also have a Quiet Room, where we or the vet talk to the people during a worst-case scenario. There are two essential papers given out when a pet dies. They are "Prayer at the Death of a Pet" and "The Rainbow Bridge."

These are classics that are handed from pet lover to pet lover in a chain of caring and support. This chain keeps growing and growing, as our society recognizes more and more the profound ways our best friends enrich our lives and remain in our hearts forever. Someone may give you the "Prayer at the Death of a Pet" or "The Rainbow Bridge" someday, if you seek grief

counseling during the illness or after the death of a
beloved pet. If someday you feel the need to visit our
Quiet Room at Friends Helping Friends and circum-
stances make that impossible, I'd like to share these
with you now.

I cannot read "The Rainbow Bridge" without getting
a lump in my throat.

THE RAINBOW BRIDGE

There is a bridge connecting Heaven and Earth.
  It is called the
Rainbow Bridge because of its many colors.
  Just this side of the
Rainbow Bridge there is a land of meadows,
  hills and valleys with lush green grass. When a
  beloved pet dies, the pet
goes to this place. There is always food and
water and warm spring weather. The old and frail
  animals are
young again. Those who are maimed are made whole
  again.
They play all day with each other.

There is only one thing missing.
They are not with their special person who loved
  them on Earth.
So, each day they run and play until the day comes
  when one
suddenly stops playing and looks up!
The nose twitches! The ears are up! The eyes are
  staring!
And this one suddenly runs from the group!

You have been seen, and when you and your special
  friend meet,
you take him or her in your arms and embrace. Your
  face is
kissed again and again and again; and you look once
  more into
the eyes of your trusting pet.

Then you can cross the Rainbow Bridge together
never again to be separated.

PRAYER AT THE DEATH OF A PET

Lord God,
to those who have never had a pet,
this prayer will sound strange,
but to You, Lord of All Life and Creator of All
  Creatures,
it will be understandable.
My heart is heavy
as I face the loss in death of my beloved ———
who was so much a part of my life.

This pet made my life more enjoyable
and gave me cause to laugh
and to find joy in her company.
I remember the fidelity and loyalty of this pet
and will miss her being with me.
From her I learned many lessons, such as the quality
  of naturalness
and the unembarrassed request for affection.
In caring for her daily needs,
I was taken up and out of my own self-needs
and thus learned to service another.

May the death of this creature of Yours
remind me that death comes to all of us,
animal and human,
and that it is the natural passage for all life.
May ——— sleep on
in an eternal slumber in Your Godly care
as all creation awaits the fullness of liberation.

Amen.

—Alan Novak, Friends Helping Friends

CHAPTER NINE

Of Love and Death

Dogs' lives are too short. Their only fault, really.
        —Agnes Sligh Turnbull

I have sometimes thought of the final cause of dogs having such short lives and I am quite satisfied it is in compassion to the human race; for if we suffer so much in losing a dog after an acquaintance of ten or twelve years, what would it be if they were to live double that time?
        —Sir Walter Scott

The one best place to bury a good dog is in the heart of his master.
        —Ben Hur Lampman

Megan's Gift

I noticed her out of the corner of my eye. Megan was in the backyard, chasing after birds, when she tripped ever so slightly. I decided the stumble must have been from a rock or a depression in the grass, because when I looked up from my work, she was running around again as though nothing had happened.

A week later, I caught her limping, almost imperceptibly, on her right front leg. A little bruise, perhaps, or maybe a small scrape from a fall in the woods? An ordinary pet owner might not have thought twice about such a thing. But the minute I saw the limp, I suspected something was wrong. And I could feel myself trembling as the awful conviction started to take hold of me. "She has bone cancer," I thought.

I called out to her, and as she happily bounded over to me, she seemed a robust, perfectly healthy fourteen-year-old golden retriever. But something was telling me otherwise. I immediately opened the door to my Jeep and rushed her to my office for a thorough examination.

The X-rays of her leg confirmed what I already feared. As I held the pictures up to the light, I could see the faint beginnings of cancer in her carpus. I looked at Megan, my remarkably kind and devoted dog, and then back at the pictures in my hand. I started to cry. Megan had seen me through so much. Had time flown so fast?

My awakening as a veterinarian began the day I met Megan eleven years earlier. She had the worst case of heartworm disease I had ever seen. A friend of mine had found Megan in the little Yankee town of Jaffrey, New Hampshire, not far from Peterborough, where I had my first job as a veterinarian. Day after day, the forlorn creature would wander lethargically outside my friend's office, looking for a handout and a shred of kindness. Every few steps, she would collapse to the ground in paroxysms of coughing, then struggle to get up, and, a few steps later, collapse again. There were no identification tags, no collar, nothing to suggest that once, long ago, someone had loved and cared for her. She was alone, sick and helpless.

Eleven years ago, I had looked into the tired, pleading eyes of the dearest face I had ever seen and made a promise: "If you make it, I'll keep you."

Megan not only made it, miraculously surviving a long, dangerous treatment for heartworm, she became a life-giving force, a canine Florence Nightingale with a healing power far beyond anything I had learned in veterinary school.

One night when I brought home a lamb that had been viciously attacked by a pack of wild dogs, Megan licked her, cleaned her, nuzzled her, and slept alongside her all night long. The next morning, Megan awakened me and led me toward the living room, where the lamb stood on sturdy legs, *baa*ing, as Megan wagged her tail furiously. The next day, we were able to send the lamb home to her farm. I say *we* because there was never any doubt in my mind about why the lamb recovered so quickly. Somehow, with a simple outpouring of love, Megan had touched the very essence of the other creature to cause a physical transformation within.

I witnessed this miracle again and again. When a Maine coon mother was incapacitated by emergency surgery, having lost two of her kittens, it was Megan who licked the amniotic fluid from the two surviving kittens, acting as surrogate mother. A ferret near death from liver disease, pathetically emaciated from toxins, recovered after a week of Megan playfully pushing him to and fro with her snout, responding with soft nuzzles when the ferret bit her nose.

When a hunter accidentally shot his German short-haired pointer in the abdomen, Megan, without a word from me, followed the hunter to the waiting room during emergency surgery and rested her head in his lap. Later, when I approached her and said, "Megan, I need you," she instinctively raised her paw to my needle as I set up the blood transfusion that saved the pointer's life.

Megan's gift, little by little, began to touch and renew my own spirits. I realized there was a part of my nature that had been buried by the rigid rationalism instilled in me in veterinary school. There, animals weren't so much living creatures as "cases." Megan had awakened in me the kind of kinship with animals that I had known instinctively as a child.

Watching her nurse other animals, I began to understand that the elemental bonds of nature were more powerful than anything the scientific establishment had to offer. In those bonds were the strands of love, of kindness, and of physical and spiritual healing—the strands of life itself.

Now the prognosis was terrible for my sweet, gentle friend and teacher. Some veterinarians recommend radiation and chemotherapy, along with amputation, to arrest the spread of the disease. But Megan was already getting on in years, and I couldn't put her through such suffering. I wanted to let her go with dignity, with her mind and body intact.

That night I dragged myself home, dreading the task of breaking the news to my wife, Barbara. Megan had been part of our lives since the very beginning, and had even been present at our backyard wedding. She had served as a kind of maid of honor, wearing a

big pink bow that matched the trim on Barbara's dress,
and parking herself between Barbara and me during the
ceremony—where she promptly fell asleep!

Megan was lying in front of us by the fireplace as I
told Barbara. Together, we cried softly, and told Megan
how much we loved her. She just lay there looking at
us, her eyes knowing, accepting what was said.

Barbara and I talked about our options and agreed it
was best not to do anything "heroic." Instead, we threw
ourselves into the task of making Megan as comfortable
as we could. Barbara made her home-cooked organic
meals, and I carefully regulated her medication, putting
her on natural painkillers and anti-inflammatory
agents.

But the truth was that we didn't need to *do* anything
for Megan. Just as she had nursed others, she quite
naturally started taking care of herself. And as I observed her over the next weeks and months, I realized
that through her illness, this dog, who had awakened
me to a new way of relating to my patients, was still
acting as my teacher. In subtle but important ways, she
was still showing me how to *live*, even as she was dying.

I watched amazed as she began to regulate her own
activity level. As her cancer progressed, she started
slowing down on the walks we took down a nearby
country path. Where we used to take one-and-a-half-
mile strolls, now after three-quarters of a mile she
would stop, sniff some bushes or watch a butterfly, and
rest for a while. If Barbara and I kept on walking,
Megan would simply stand on the side of the road sniffing the bushes until we returned, then walk back home
with us. After a few months, she started going half a
mile, then a quarter of a mile, until finally our walks
were nothing more than a slow meander up the driveway.

Even more miraculously, as the tumor grew bigger, Megan sought out a natural spring in the back of our house, where she would stick her front leg in the mud and soak it. Instinctively, she had discovered a method of pain relief that has been known for centuries. Mud packs are used in many cultures to heal inflammation, and they are also an old treatment for cancer. No one urged Megan toward this healing method. She just knew.

She also seemed to know that her time was growing short, but she didn't appear to mind at all. Four months had passed since I first detected the tumor, and little by little, she had slowed down to the point that she rarely went out anymore. Around the house, she would hobble a few yards, wagging her tail and sniffing occasionally at a bug or a ball of dust. But mostly she would lie on the floor, drifting off into long naps, while Barbara and I went about our business.

As Megan slowed down, I was growing increasingly anxious. I had a three-week lecture series coming up in Norway that had been arranged over a year before. But I didn't want to leave Megan, I *couldn't* leave Megan in her final days. For weeks I was in turmoil. My only recourse was to ask Megan. Every day, I would look at her and say, "I don't want to put you to sleep when you're happy and enjoying life. But I can't cancel this lecture. What should I do?" Megan never seemed to give me an answer.

I had tried to postpone the lectures, but too many people were involved to make that possible. Now, all I could do was make the final preparations for leaving, and hope that Megan would hold out until Barbara and I returned.

As the day of our departure grew closer, I was beside myself. "Megan, I *can't* leave you, you know that!" I would say. Our eyes would meet and she would wag her tail a little in response.

All the arrangements for Norway were made. A reliable dog-sitter, someone Megan knew, had been lined up; my partner had instructions not to do anything heroic in my absence. Finally, I resigned myself to the fact that I might have to leave Megan without saying a final good-bye. The loving companion that had been with me for so long might have to end her days alone.

But even now, Megan came through to teach me one last lesson. The day before Barbara and I were to leave, we awoke to find Megan breathing heavily, stretched out on the floor at the foot of our bed where she always slept. Her eyes were open, but her body was so leaden that she couldn't lift up her head.

I knelt down with my face next to hers and looked into her eyes. "Megan," I said gently. "This is it, isn't it?"

She had already given her answer. Barbara was crying quietly on the bed as I turned to Megan to acknowledge what was in our hearts. Megan knew. She knew we were leaving, knew we might never see each other again—and so in a final act of love, she was choosing to leave ahead of us.

We sat hugging for a while, all three of us, and then I went downstairs to my study to get the hypodermic needle. When I came back up, Barbara was on the floor with Megan's head resting comfortably in her lap.

For a few moments I sat immobile, staring at Barbara and Megan with the syringe in my hand, not wanting to face the inevitable. Somehow Megan must have heard my thoughts and seen my inner conflict. Because before I could say or do a thing, she lifted her right paw ever so slightly to receive the injection. It was the same paw I had used to save her eleven years ago.

That gesture was a summation of her special legacy. As I gently inserted the needle, I remembered Megan on the day after we first met, when she stretched out her paw to accept the IV that saved her from heartworm. And I remembered her a few years later, when she willingly stretched out that same paw to give her life-saving blood in a transfusion to a wounded dog. In the end, it was clear she had died as she had lived—still reaching out to others.

Within seconds it was over. As Barbara cradled her head in her arms, Megan let out a deep sigh and died. We carried her out back and dug a grave, where we buried her and bid our silent farewells.

Yet that good-bye wasn't the end for us. Megan's tremendous impact on my life lives on. I think of her almost daily. Her knowing eyes and loving embrace of others come to mind as I go about my work. Sometimes I become so busy that I fear I'm about to lose my perspective on who I am and what my mission really is. But in those moments of pressure and distraction, the memory of Megan brings me back to true reality—the reality that love is the only force that can make us thoroughly sensitive and responsive to the needs of others, animal and human alike.

—*Allen Schoen*

A Little Dog Angel

High up in the courts of heaven today
A little dog angel waits;
With the other angels he will not play,
But he sits alone at the gates.
"For I know my master will come," says he,
"And when he comes he will call for me."

The other angels pass him by
As they hurry towards the throne,
And he watches them with a wistful eye
As he sits at the gates alone.
"But I know if I just wait patiently
That someday my master will call for me."

And his master, down on the earth below,
As he sits in his easy chair,
Forgets sometimes, and whispers low
To the dog, who is not there.
And the little dog angel cocks his ears,
And dreams that his master's voice he hears.

And when at last his master waits
Outside in the dark and cold,
For the hand of death to open the door,
That leads to those courts of gold,
He will hear a sound through the gathering dark,
A little dog angel's bark.

—*Norah Holland*

Nero

My beloved dog, Nero, died on April 1, 1995. He was fifteen years old. He was a gift from my mother when I was eighteen, and she was ill with terminal cancer. She bought me Nero to cheer me up and take my mind off her illness. As it turned out, she was very attached to him, too. He was supposed to be a cocker spaniel and poodle cross, a miniature that would grow no larger than twelve inches in length. However, he was, depending on how you looked at it, either the most fascinating mixture of Scottie, German shepherd, dachshund, and pit bull or the ugliest dog you have ever seen.

Nero had real attitude . . . he did precisely what he wanted and the only tricks he did were ones he learned himself, like opening the fridge door with his paw and stealing steaks off a hot grill. He was very brave and would not back down from anyone. He hated it when I put him in sissy dog clothes . . . growling at me ferociously. He bit several people on the nose, but these were people that stuck their face into his without invitation. He loved me unconditionally, and when I brought home a second dog, when Nero was ten, he begrudgingly accepted and grew to love Skooter.

Nero was with me the night my mom died. He was there throughout my turbulent twenties. He was there when my heart was broken and when all the love I had was transferred to this shaggy black creature. When I met the man I would later marry, Nero accepted him and welcomed him into our lives. Nero was there on my wedding day, in my official wedding portrait. When I became pregnant, Nero would lie with me, his chin resting on my ever-expanding belly. He was the first to feel the baby kick.

On February 3, the day my daughter was born, Nero started medication for his arthritic back. He became listless, yet he managed to drag himself to greet the newest member of the household. After grunting his approval, he settled into the nursery and watched over the baby. As he got worse, many people thought the kind thing to do would be to have him put to sleep. With some dogs that may be the case, but Nero always threw a fit at the vet's office, acting as if it were his last visit there, and the thought of actually taking him to be euthanized was just too hard. The last couple of weeks were tough, but the night before he died we bathed him and set him on a blanket. He crawled into the baby's room, and that is where we found him, having gone to his eternal rest.

I miss him so very much, as does his buddy, Skooter. I could not think of a greater tribute to Nero than to give another loving creature a good home. So after a few weeks, we went to the animal shelter and picked up a new friend for Skooter. Sheppy is his name, an Australian cattle dog that was abandoned on the highway. He is not a replacement but an enhancement to our lives.

I believe there is a place in heaven for dogs (and other beloved pets) to rejoin their loved ones, and I know that is where my Nero is, probably chasing cars made of smoked ham and mailmen made of salami!

In closing, these are a few of the things that made Nero special: his morning coffee, light with two Sweet'n Lows; the way he barked at statues of horses and cows; the way he rode shotgun in the car, *everywhere*, even in the dead of winter when he would jump in the backseat, curl up, and sleep while I was doing errands in the mall; his favorite toy, a chocolate-scented rubber replica of a human foot; and the love and devotion he gave me for fifteen great years. I only hope I did well by you, my "number one baby boy."

—*Martin & Rosemarie*

Our Baby Girl

SABRE
A ROTTWEILER BITCH
BLACK AND TAN
107 POUNDS
DECEMBER 26, 1986–NOVEMBER 1, 1995

Sabre was our first dog ever. My husband was forty-seven and I was thirty-five when we went to see a seven-week-old litter. We had never seen rottie puppies before and were astonished at their size so young. Sabre was the alpha female (fourteen pounds) and chose us by tagging along after my husband and chewing his shoe-strings every chance she got. What a delightful, opinionated, hard-headed little angel. Soon enough she came to understand a lot of English, and she quickly taught us rottie-speak.

Obedience training was a chore, as it took us two courses of ten weeks each before she even qualified in basic obedience. She did well at the weekly classes in group, but graduation was solo. On stage by herself, with all eyes on her, she hammed it up. "What's heel? What's sit?" The second ten-week course was the same; and at graduation, the instructors took pity on me and barely passed her. They knew she was reliable in class with her group, but being on stage alone brought out the nut in her. I was so embarrassed, but later realized that this was part of what made her so special.

Sabre could have been the National Rottweiler Breed poster child. She was so gentle and loving. The children in the neighborhood adored her and she them. They were her babies. And the smaller the child, the more gentle she was. When one of her babies cried, so did she. We took Sabre every place possible. Everyone she met was a potential toy. And the wiggles! The hind end wiggled the dog. Spoiled rotten she was, and there could be no popcorn in the house unless it had butter on it. No margarine for her, thank you!

From stalking games to standing on our feet, she made our home hers and ensured everything was in proper Rottweiler order for almost nine years. A ride in the car sent her into convulsions of ecstasy, especially if it ended in a visit to my mother (Grandma). She knew the route and would start squealing about a half mile from Mom's house. Oh, how she loved her grandma. Even her daily walk on a leash around the neighborhood was reason to bounce for joy. She loved doing anything or going anywhere with her mommy or daddy.

In March 1995, she started limping on the left foreleg. We thought (at eight years) it was a little arthritis and dosed her at night with aspirin. It helped. She woke up one morning near the end of April and was on three legs. The left foreleg could not touch the floor without her crying in terrible pain. A trip to the vet and an X-ray revealed osteosarcoma (bone cancer) of the left humerus. Prognosis was terminal in about six months. We put her on antibiotics on the off-chance that we were dealing with a bone infection, since it presents the same way on X-ray. Surprisingly, she improved in a few days and was romping around and acting silly like before.

She did pretty well until July when the limping started again. We added five milligrams of prednisone per day to the pharmacopeia; and again she bounced back, but only for a few weeks. It was a gradual downhill slide after that, and we had to increase her prednisone, until she was up to twenty milligrams per day. Her liver became enlarged. Her mind was alert, and she was still very interested in family activities up until the day before we sent her to puppy heaven. She couldn't get around very well. Going outside to potty wiped her out. Her appetite faded, and so did her interest in life. She couldn't get comfortable her last day. Bone cancer pain is excruciating. It tore my husband's heart to shreds.

We held her and cried that afternoon before the last trip to the vet. We held her and whispered sweet nothings into her ears as she went to sleep for the last time. We held her in overwhelming silent anguish, as her footpads turned cold—not wanting to make any noise to upset clients in the waiting room and not wanting to finally leave her.

I trimmed some fur from her neck for something to touch and remember. We arranged for cremation and the return of her ashes. Sabre will be with us always,

and we look forward to the time when we will see her
again.

—*Linda and Jim*

Missing Our Dogs

Old men miss many dogs.
They only live a dozen years, if that
And by the time you're sixty, there are several
The names of which evoke remembering smiles.
You see them in your mind, heads cocked and seated.
You see them by your bed, or in the rain,
Or sleeping by the fire by night
And always dying.

You are young but they are old. They go,
The German shepherd and the poodle,
The bassett hound and mutt.
They are remembered like departed children
Though they gave vastly more than ever they took,
And finally you're seeing dogs that look like them.
They pass you in the street but never turn
Although it seems they should, their faces so familiar.
Old men miss many dogs.

—*Steve Allen*

The Power of the Dog

There is sorrow enough in the natural way
From men and women to fill our day;
And when we are certain of sorrow in store,
Why do we always arrange for more?
Brothers and Sisters, I bid you beware
Of giving your heart to a dog to tear.

Buy a pup and your money will buy
Love unflinching that cannot lie—
Perfect passion and worship fed
By a kick in the ribs or a pat on the head.
Nevertheless it is hardly fair
To risk your heart for a dog to tear.

When the fourteen years which Nature permits
Are closing in asthma, or tumor, or fits,
And the vet's unspoken prescription runs
To lethal chambers or loaded guns,
Then you will find—it's your own affair—
But . . . you've given your heart to a dog to tear.

When the body that lived at your single will,
With its whimper of welcome, is stilled (how still!)
When the spirit that answered your every mood
Is gone—wherever it goes—for good
You will discover how much you care,
And will give your heart to a dog to tear.

We've sorrow enough in the natural way,
When it comes to burying in Christian clay.
Our loves are not given, but only lent,
At compound interest of cent per cent.

Though it is not always the case, I believe,
That the longer we've kept 'em, the more do we
  grieve.

For, when debts are payable, right or wrong,
A short time loan is as bad as a long—
So why in—Heaven (before we are there)
Should we give our hearts to a dog to tear?

                              —*Rudyard Kipling*

Friday: A Son's Story

BIG HEADED GULLUTE
BIG HEADED MONSTER
CIRCUS DOG
FRI DOG
FRY
FRYGUY
FRYMASTER
FRYMONSTER
FRYSTER
FUR FACE
GRANDOG
HAPPY DOG
HOUND DOGGIE

HOUNDSTER
KING FRYDAY
KING BUDDIE
KING DOGGIE
KING BOY
LEAPER DOG
MR. FEROCIOUS
MR. PATIENCE
MR. FUR BETWEEN YOUR TOES CAN'T
  WAIT FOR ME TO GET READY TO Go
  OUTSIDE
MY LITTLE BUDDY
MR. POLITE BOY
PRANCER DOG
RUFFA DUFFA
SHOVEL PAW
SILLY MANAMULE
SNOW DOG
SQUIRREL HUNTER
THE HUNTER DOG
THE KING
THE SWAMP THING

MADE Us LAUGH
MADE Us CRY
MADE Us WORRY
MADE Us HAPPY
MADE Us SAD
MADE Us WONDER
MADE Us SMILE

WE ARE FORTUNATE
HE WAS FORTUNATE
HE Is THE KING

I MISS HIM
WE MISS HIM

I AM SAD

—*Scott Forbis*

Koblenz

On a rainy cold morning in July, the police knocked at our front door to tell us our shop had been broken into. Koblenz, our fourteen-year-old German shepherd, got a bit excited, barked, and dropped to the floor. The vet was very kind, so he called and examined Koblenz. He could not tell my husband, as they were inseparable, so he came to me with tears in his eyes and said, "He has had a stroke and will not survive."

After getting the tears from my face, I thought we would see how he goes. That night he was worse. He lay on the bathroom floor unable to move, so I had made my decision. I couldn't let him suffer. So in the morning I decided to see the vet. Not wanting to leave Koblenz alone, I took some pillows and a blanket and lay on the concrete floor with my hand on his paw. Every time I took it away, he would try and raise his head and look at me. By 3:00 A.M., I knew it was soon.

He dragged himself into our bedroom and lay down beside the bed, so I went to bed still keeping my hand on him so he was not alone. We did not sleep. We just lay there listening to his breathing.

My husband could not bring it to terms that Koblenz was very ill, so he went to have a shower. Five A.M. came and Koblenz lifted his head right up and stared into my eyes (that I will never forget). I yelled for my husband to come, then Koblenz lay down his head and took his last breath. We made a box, dug a hole in the garden, and buried him with all his toys, pillow, and blanket. We cried so much I thought we would never stop. We later found that he also had cancer, but we never would of known because all he ever wanted to do was make us happy. So his headstone, which we had made with his photo, says it all:

KEYWAYS "COBY" KOBLENZ
In Times of Good, Bad, Happy & Sad, By our side you always remained. You gave us sunshine when it wasn't there, For this we forever love you.

And every week we put on fresh flowers and talk to him every day. We still and always will love him ever so much. Koblenz—German shepherd, RIP.

—Anonymous from the Virtual Pet Cemetery

Farewell to a Rottweiler

Today I held you as you breathed your last. It hurt so much to let you go. As I cried into your fur, you turned those loving, trusting eyes on me and asked me to help you. I couldn't ignore your last request, not after all you have given to me. You were the most loving, wonderful rottie in the world. Even though I hurt, I know you don't. I'll always remember your wonderful life, the waddling fluff who tripped over his feet, to the loving, supportive companion of later years. All you wanted was to be near me—playing, loving, or just being together quietly. I'll miss our little talks and you underfoot as I cleaned the house. You protected me from buzzards and planes flying in the sky; warned me when noisy vehicles and the ice cream truck were near; sang with the sirens of emergency vehicles, even those on TV. When your daddy left, you were there for me, giving me all the love in your big heart. No one could ask for a better nurse. You wouldn't leave my side to eat or drink—I had to bring your bowls into the bedroom. You had so much love to give, I let you become a therapy dog. You only got to make one trip but you made a big impact on lots of people. Then you became ill. I thought you could bring love to others, and I prayed so hard you'd get well. But the Lord has called you to the Rainbow Bridge. I know you hurt no more; you're free and happy as you romp with the other dogs at the bridge. Wait there for me, Prince. I'll come for you one day. Go with God, baby. I love you so much, and I'll miss you. You'll always be in my heart.

Till we meet again, baby.
Prince Damien II
April 21, 1987–June 10, 1996

—Susan Taylor

Rosy

I didn't see your notes until after we had been home a while on Friday. Since you hadn't said anything before I left, I thought you had decided against it; and Jim was silent. Now he read the notes and, saying little to one another, we agreed to it.

That evening she was, as she has been, underfoot and bumping about but now of course it didn't matter. At one point Jim said: "She's tickling my legs, make her stop!" and we laughed. Despite a light rain, I cooked on the grill and down the steps she came; her nose never failed her. She ate her dinner and begged for ours. Contrary to your usual admonitions, I gave her all the scraps as we left. I hesitated for a moment to leave her alone but the alternatives seemed unnecessary.

In the morning I called the hospital: "Bring her in before one o'clock, no need to wait." Jim got ready, and I went back to the house. I found her asleep amid the remains of last night's excess. Rousing her as gently as I could, I saw she wagged for me. I carried her up to the backyard and put her down. Another wag and a shake, and she went about "beagle business." I left her alone and began our own seventeen-year morning ritual: wash the bowl, fill with clean water, fix the food (these days warmed in the microwave—still daring, she liked it on the raw side), and then, and only then, could the coffee be started. After a time she made her way back in, drank noisily, and before breakfast had an excellent roll every which way on the dining room rug. I carefully wiped her eyes. Jim was here, and it was time to go.

I picked her up and carried her out to the car. When I opened the door the movement startled her blind eyes and she cringed as she had taken to doing. I wept as I tried to reassure her while yet affirming the rightness of what we were about to do. Jim drove with the windows wide open; she was held tight and rested uncharacteristically easy in my arms, her nose lifted just a bit to sniff the breeze. Choral music, which she couldn't hear, lulled Jim and me.

At the hospital, they offered to take her as we completed the paperwork. But I said no and held her a bit tighter and a little closer. She never resisted. They offered us a room but I said "you can take her anytime" and they did. A young woman came in and quietly petting her asked, "What's her name?" I said "Rosy," and let her go. One ear flopped down, and she was carried away. Back in the car, the lovely *Gloria* had ended; but it seemed then, and it seems now, that the notes, like Rosy, will always be playing somewhere.

At 1:30 I went back and took her home one more time. They wrapped her in towels and placed her in the wicker bed. I packed her bowl; her "beagle bag"; and all the leashes (how many leashes does a dog need when God knows she never heeled to them anyhow); all the balls and toys of her youth (how raucous, feisty, exasperating, and unending it appeared); and finally all the colored scarves of her "hot dog" glory days (how funny, silly, crazy, improbable, yet charming they truly were).

Jim came once again, and we dug the place up in the arch of the tree as we always said we would. Then . . . "in the wheelbarrow up to the hole, her fur took the sun."*

—Johann Klodzen

* From *Another Dog's Death*, by John Updike.

Lady Margaret

FEBRUARY 24, 1994–APRIL 28, 1996
UNTIL WE MEET AGAIN ON THE RAINBOW BRIDGE.

I still see your joyous self
Bounding beside your beloved Sasha—
Comical hips & tail twitching
Voice raised in counterpoint
After the sly squirrels that always elude you both.

The thrill was ever in the chase.

I still feel your sweet, warm tongue in my ear
When the morning alarm goes off:
"Time to get up, Mom; time to begin, Mom;
Let me scootch onto your pillow, Mom;
I'll charm my way into your dreams, Mom."

The peace was ever in your love.

And now I hear your contented murmurs
Groans and sighs in angel-sleep
As you continue your happy trek with
The sly squirrels leading you
Into the dark woods where I cannot follow.

The joy was ever in the Sheltie-Talk.

—*Joan Samuelson*

The Last Will and Testament of an Extremely Distinguished Dog

I, Silverdene Emblem O'Neill (familiarly known to my family, friends, and acquaintances as Blemie), because the burden of my years and infirmities is heavy upon me, and I realize the end of my life is near, do hereby bury my last will and testament in the mind of my Master. He will not know it is there until I am dead. Then, remembering me in his loneliness, he will suddenly know of this testament, and I ask him then to inscribe it as a memorial to me.

I have little in the way of material things to leave. Dogs are wiser than men. They do not set great store upon things. They do not waste their days hoarding property. They do not ruin their sleep worrying about how to keep the objects they have, and to obtain the objects they have not. There is nothing of value I have to bequeath except my love and faith. These I leave to all those who loved me, to my Master and Mistress, who I know will mourn me most, to Freeman, who has been so good to me, to Cyn and Roy and Willie and Naomi and— But if I should list all those who have loved me it would force my Master to write a book. Perhaps it is vain of me to boast when I am so near death, which returns all beasts and vanities to dust, but I have always been an extremely lovable dog.

I ask my Master and Mistress to remember me always, but not to grieve for me too long. In my life I have tried to be a comfort to them in time of sorrow, and a reason for added joy in their happiness. It is painful for me to think that even in death I should cause them pain. Let them remember that while no dog has ever had a happier life (and this I owe to their love and care for me), now that I have grown blind and deaf and lame, and even my sense of smell fails me so that a rabbit could be right under my nose and I might not know, my pride has sunk to a sick, bewildered humiliation. I feel life is taunting me with having over-lingered my welcome. It is time I said good-bye, before I become too sick a burden on myself and on those who love me. It will be sorrow to leave them, but not a sorrow to die. Dogs do not fear death as men do. We accept it as a part of life, not as something alien and terrible which destroys life. What may come after death, who knows? I would like to believe with those of my fellow Dalmatians who are devout Mohammedans, that there is a Paradise where one is always young and full-bladdered; where all the day one dillies and dallies with an enormous multitude of houris, beautifully spotted; where jackrabbits that run fast but not too fast (like the houris) are as the sands of the desert; where each blissful hour is mealtime; where in long evenings there are a million fireplaces with logs forever burning, and one curls oneself up and blinks into the flames and nods and dreams, remembering the old brave days on earth, and the love of one's Master and Mistress.

I am afraid this is too much for even such a dog as I am to expect. But peace, at least, is certain. Peace and long rest for weary old heart and head and limbs, and eternal sleep in the earth I have loved so well. Perhaps, after all, this is best.

One last request I earnestly make. I have heard my Mistress say, "When Blemie dies we must never have another dog. I love him so much I could never love another one." Now I would ask her, for love of me, to have another. It would be a poor tribute to my memory never to have a dog again. What I would like to feel is that, having once had me in the family, now she cannot live without a dog! I have never had a jealous spirit. I have always held that most dogs are good (and one cat, the black one I have permitted to share the living room rug during the evenings, whose affection I have tolerated in a kindly spirit, and in rare sentimental moods, even reciprocated a trifle). Some dogs, of course, are better than others. Dalmatians, naturally, as everyone knows, are best. So I suggest a Dalmatian as my successor. He can hardly be as well bred or as well mannered or as distinguished and handsome as I was in my prime. My Master and Mistress must not ask the impossible. But he will do his best, I am sure, and even his inevitable defects will help by comparison to keep my memory green. To him I bequeath my collar and leash and my overcoat and raincoat, made to order in 1929 at Hermès in Paris. He never can wear them with the distinction I did, walking around the Place Vendome, or later along Park Avenue, all eyes fixed on me in admiration; but again I am sure he will do his utmost not to appear a mere gauche provincial dog. Here on the ranch, he may prove himself quite worthy of comparison, in some respects. He will, I presume, come closer to jackrabbits than I have been able to in recent years. And, for all his faults, I hereby wish him the happiness I know will be his in my old home.

One last word of farewell, dear Master and Mistress. Whenever you visit my grave, say to yourselves with regret but also with happiness in your hearts at the remembrance of my long happy life with you: "Here lies one who loved us and whom we loved." No matter how deep my sleep I shall hear you, and not all the power of death can keep my spirit from wagging a grateful tail.

—Eugene O'Neill

Grateful acknowledgment is made for permission to reprint
from the following:

Page 5: "A Dog's Home Is Many Hearths" by Roberta Sandler. Copyright © Roberta Sandler. Reprinted with permission of the author.

Page 8: "Maxie" by Anonymous. Taken from LavaMind's Virtual Pet
Cemetery, http://www.lavamind.com/pet.html. The Virtual Pet Cemetery is a unique cyber graveyard for pets. Over the years, this special
place has grown to become one of the world's best known and largest
online burial grounds. Thousands of visitors from all over the world
visit the cemetery every day to read and share epitaphs.

Page 9: "The Never-Ending Dog" by Jill Francisco. Reprinted by
permission of Warner Books, Inc. New York, New York, U.S.A. From
Mutts: America's Dogs by Brian Kilcommons and Mike Capuzzo. All
rights reserved.

Page 11: "Loving Lizzie" by Kitty Brown Gutstein. Reprinted with
permission from the Delta Society. The Delta Society was founded as a
nonprofit organization in 1977. Delta Society's mission is to promote
animals helping people improve their health, independence, and quality of life. Our goals are to expand public awareness of the positive
effects of animals on family health and development, reduce barriers to
enjoyment of animals in everyday life, deliver animal-assisted therapy
to more people, and increase the number of well-trained service dogs
available to people with disabilities. For more information please con-
tact the Delta Society at: 289 Perimeter Road East, Renton, WA
98055-1329, (206) 226-7357.

Page 37: "A Gift for Eternity" by Bill Tarrant. From The Magic of Dogs
by Bill Tarrant. Copyright © 1995 by Bill Tarrant. Reprinted with
permission of the Lyons Press.

Page 50: "The Minister's Guru" by Gary Kowalski. From The Souls of
Animals by Gary Kowalski. Copyright © 1991 by Gary Kowalski. Ex-
cerpted with permission of Stillpoint Publishing.

Page 53: "Chip" by Kimberlee L. Lippencott. Reprinted by permission of the author. Adapted from "In Loving Memory" by Kimberlee
L. Lippencott. From Paws for Thought: How Animals Enrich Our Lives—

Page 264: "Nero" by Martin and Rosemarie. Taken from LavaMind's Virtual Pet Cemetery, http://www.lavamind.com/pet.html.

Page 266: "Our Baby Girl" by Linda and Jim. Taken from LavaMind's Virtual Pet Cemetery, http://www.lavamind.com/pet.html.

Page 269: "Missing Our Dogs" by Steve Allen. From *The Dogs of Our Lives: Heartwarming Reminiscences of Canine Companions* compiled by Louise Goodyear Murray. Copyright © 1995 by Louise Goodyear Murray. A Citadel Press Book. Reprinted by arrangement with Carol Publishing Group.

Page 273: "Koblenz" by Anonymous. Taken from LavaMind's Virtual Pet Cemetery, http://www.lavamind.com/pet.html.

Page 275: "Farewell to a Rottweiler" by Susan Taylor. Reprinted by permission of the author. First published in Farokh's Dog Page, http://www.dogpage.mcf.com.

Page 276: "Rosy" by Johann Klodzen. Reprinted with permission of the author. First published in Dead Pet Page, http://www.geocities.com/Heartland/4139/cemetery.html.

Page 278: "Lady Margaret" by Joan Samuelson. Reprinted with permission of the author. First published in Farokh's Dog Page, http://www.dogpage.mcf.com.

About the Authors

Four times nominated for the Pulitzer Prize, Michael Capuzzo writes a nationally syndicated pet column that appears in *Newsday*, the *Philadelphia Inquirer*, *Rocky Mountain News*, and numerous other newspapers. He is the author of *Wild Things* and *Mutts: America's Dogs*. Teresa Banik Capuzzo writes feature stories for the *Philadelphia Inquirer* and *Philadelphia Daily News*. She was the chief researcher for an *Inquirer* Pulitzer Prize–winning series and the book *America: What Went Wrong?* The Capuzzos, who live on a farm in southern New Jersey, are coauthors of *Cat Caught My Heart*, the companion volume to *Our Best Friends*.

Printed in the United States
by Baker & Taylor Publisher Services